# DASH Diet Mediterranean Solution

Guide for Beginners to Weight Loss with Meal Plan and Meal Prep.
The Hypertension Action Plan and Health Plan to Detox with Recipes and Cookbook.

# TABLE OF CONTENTS

such, any inattention, use, or misuse of the information in question by the reader will render any resulting actions solely under their purview. There are no scenarios in which the publisher or the original author of this work can be in any fashion deemed liable for any hardship or damages that may befall them after undertaking information described herein.

Additionally, the information in the following pages is intended only for informational purposes and should thus be thought of as universal. As befitting its nature, it is presented without assurance regarding its prolonged validity or interim quality. Trademarks that are mentioned are done without written consent and can in no way be considered an endorsement from the trademark holder.

# Introduction

Your grandmother probably said it – you are what you eat.

It may be one of the most accurate aphorisms ever uttered. And it doesn't take a genius to figure out that if you're eating low-quality junk food, your body is not going to be operating at an optimal level.

The health of your immune system, your organs, bodily functions and the clarity of your mind all depend on getting the right nutrients while keeping harmful toxins out. While consuming a diet full of sugar, salt, fatty second rate meat and empty carbs in white bread might keep you alive over the short term, it's clearly not the best fuel to keep you going. These kinds of junk foods will literally rust out your body and put wear and tear on it the way fueling a nice new car with 100% ethanol would over time.

Consuming unhealthy foods e.g. junk food leads to weight gain. Thus, the increase in weight, the body develops many problems. Among these is a decreasing ability to process carbohydrates. This comes from overloading the system with simple sugars. Imagine driving a car like a mad man, racing all over town and driving over bumps and through ruts, without ever changing the oil. The car will wear out very quickly. In the early stages, the car can handle the abuse, but eventually, things start breaking down, and the breakdowns kind of reinforce each other until the car is done. This is kind of what happens to your metabolic system when it's constantly bombarded with sugar. When you're young, you can withstand a lot more abuse. You can eat endless pizzas, French fries and drink sodas without any ill effects. However, as you age the damage begins to sink in. Eventually, diabetes and high blood pressure, and maybe even heart attacks and cancer result.

There are many diets out there, and we know that fruits and vegetables provide healthy nutrients is important for all aspects of health. We've also heard that avoiding bad fats helps avoid heart disease, but low-fat diets are usually unsatisfying. We've also been told that we should eat more fish.

What if you could take the two healthiest diets, and combine them together into a new better diet, that takes advantage of the latest scientific findings of nutrition and weight loss?

Meet the *Dash Diet Mediterranean Solution*, a comprehensive yet easy-to-follow diet that lets you enjoy great foods while losing weight and staying healthy!

In the early 1990s, scientists at the National Institutes of Health were studying dietary modifications in the hope of finding a natural, diet-based way to deal with hypertension or high blood pressure. Hypertension is a major risk factor for health that can lead to heart attack, stroke, bleeding aneurysms, kidney damage, and even blindness. President Franklin Delano Roosevelt died of a cerebral hemorrhage (bleeding in the brain) near the end of the second world war – and before this happened he had very high blood pressure! But back then there weren't many if any ways to treat blood pressure.

Since then many effective drugs have been developed, but in the course of their research, the scientists developed *Dietary Approaches to Stopping Hypertension* or DASH. This diet was easy to follow and based on a low-fat diet which was mainly based on eating lots of fruit and vegetables, whole grains, and low-fat proteins with some small servings of low-fat dairy. The diet also limits sodium intake. There are two versions, the standard DASH diet which limits daily sodium intake to around 2,300 mg per day, and the low-sodium DASH diet which limits sodium intake to 1,500 mg per day (the average American gets around 3,500 mg of sodium per day). While the diet wasn't designed for weight loss, since it manages food intake and if followed carefully limits calories to 2,000 calories per day, many people using it also see significant weight loss.

Now – hard to believe if you're over 40 – the 1990s were a long time ago. Since then, we've learned a lot more about diet and nutrition. As if researchers had been asleep at the wheel, they had barely noticed that people living in the Mediterranean region had very low rates of heart disease, cancer, and stroke. But very few people bothered to look in detail at what people were actually eating!

Soon the *Mediterranean Diet* was born. This dietary approach is similar to the DASH diet in its the overall approach. It encourages you to eat a lot of fruit and vegetables, with moderate protein intake. But the diets diverge on some important points. The Mediterranean diet is actually a *higher fat* diet. The diet encourages liberal use of olive oil, consumption of nuts, and consumption of high-fat fish like sardines and mackerel (although salmon isn't consumed in the Mediterranean region, you can eat plenty of it on the Mediterranean diet, because it fits in exactly with the nutrient profile).

The Mediterranean diet works because, since the time the DASH diet was discovered, researchers began to realize that the notion that fat is bad – in fact getting more fat is actually beneficial. The idea of "good fats" and "bad fats" came into being, and it turns out the Mediterranean diet is loaded with good fats. These include monounsaturated fats that are found in copious amounts in plant foods like avocados and olives (and the oils produced from them). The fats found in fish, in particular, omega-3 oils, have also been shown to reduce heart disease and stroke.

Note that the Mediterranean diet is not a diet invented by somebody – no researchers in the lab or nutritionist though it up. It's just a natural way of eating followed by the native cultures of the Mediterranean region. They happen to live in an area where all these heart-healthy foods are naturally in abundance!

Besides having some health benefits like reducing inflammation and heart attack risk, fat also helps you feel satiated when you eat. By itself, the DASH diet might strike you like a diet designed for a bird or a rabbit! But by incorporating the good fats of the Mediterranean diet, a superior approach to diet in health comes about.

Remember the DASH is designed not for losing weight, but to lower blood pressure. It does this by balancing your mineral intake. Sodium promotes fluid retention and raises blood pressure, but other minerals like potassium and magnesium have the opposite effect. You do need salt of course, but since most Americans consume far too much sodium, the balance between all these important minerals is disrupted, leading to high blood pressure. The DASH diet addresses this issue.

The DASH diet also includes a simplified system based on numbers of portions per day, rather than counting calories which makes it easy to follow.

So by combining the two diets, we get the best approach possible to improved health and weight loss. We get the DASH approach to lowering blood pressure with its simple easy-to-follow portion approach, together with the heart-healthy fats of the Mediterranean diet.

So let's get started by examining the basics of each diet individually, and then we'll develop the DASH-Mediterranean solution!

# Chapter 1: Who needs the Dash Diet Mediterranean Solution?

Over the past 50 years, people in the western world, especially in the United States have been gaining weight. The obesity epidemic is quickly becoming a public health crisis. Obesity is linked causally to multiple diseases and the more people that become obese the more people who will be sick in the coming decades. That means higher health costs for society and declining quality of life with shortened lifespans for those who are obese.

## *The importance of a Healthy Weight*

Doctors have always realized that being overweight was bad for you. This comes about from simple observation. People who are overweight run into a multitude of health problems, from simple joint problems to heart disease and cancer. In recent decades the obesity rate has been exploding. By the year 2000, researchers in the United States were already concerned with increasing obesity rates. By that time, 30% of adults and 14% of children under the age of 18 were considered obese. By 2015, 40% of adults and nearly 19% of children were suffering from obesity. What's going on?

Many factors have impacted the rise of obesity. We can start with the obvious – after 1950 Americans (and gradually other westerners) had increasing access to fast food, processed food, and junk food. While people either had to eat at home on a budget or at a sit-down restaurant prior to the second world war, by the end of the 1950s the country was full of fast in-an-out hamburger joints that let people get instant access to a meal. And the contents of the food weren't the best – in addition to a saturated fat-laden burger on a white bread bun, most would top it off with a side of deep-fried French fries loaded with salt. To wash it down, patrons would drink sugar-laden soda pop.

The grocery store evolved too, as food companies discovered ways to package carb-laden snacks that were high in salt for people to take home and eat while they sat in front of a television. They also began using artificially produced trans-fats in the snacks, since trans-fats were shelf stable and cheap. What food companies didn't know at the time was trans-fats were a major danger to heart health, as we'll see later.

Soda and other sugary products also filled the grocery shelves. The impact on obesity was gradual, as people were still relatively more physically active at the time. However, on average physical activity declined despite various health crazes that filled the passing decades. More and more people found themselves following a sedentary lifestyle, watching television and then playing video games.

Doctors then got led astray by early research into nutrition. A researcher named Ancel Keyes discovered that there was a correlation between high cholesterol and heart disease. The medical community jumped on this news, and since saturated fat consumption increases your cholesterol, they began promoting low-fat high-carb diets. By the 1980s it was received wisdom that a low-fat diet was the key to health. Even though half of the heart attacks occur in people with total cholesterol numbers below 200, doctors latched onto the idea that keeping your cholesterol below 200 was some kind of magic bullet that would prevent heart disease.

People actually listened to this advice, and as the decades wore on more carbs and less fat was consumed. Eggs were demonized on a Time magazine cover, and people reached for their super low-fat special K cereal which they ate with skim milk before heading off to aerobics. At the time, it was believed that foods that were high in cholesterol like egg yolks caused heart disease. Later it was found that in fact, dietary cholesterol has very little impact on your blood levels of cholesterol. Basically, your body makes cholesterol. When you eat it, your body makes less cholesterol. So eating an egg yolk has little impact.

Despite all of this, the health outcomes were not better. Diabetes rates have been increasing despite all the low-fat advice. Heart disease remains the number one killer, and any improvements through the years have been through new drugs (statins) and improved medical treatment, not via better nutrition. As we entered the 21st century, Americans kept getting fatter.

Over the past decade, people have been sounding alarm bells. Gary Taubes, who is actually an engineer turned nutrition expert, wrote a classic book called *Why we get fat*. This book laid out the process of digestion of sugar for the general public and explained why fat wasn't really the problem. As we'll discuss later, a blood fat called triglycerides is a major problem with heart disease, and it turns out that triglycerides although they are fat actually come from sugar. Taubes and others revealed that cutting out fat from our diets has been the root of many of the health problems we're now seeing.

## Diabetes: A Preventable Epidemic

One of the consequences of the obesity epidemic is a dramatic rise in the number of people with diabetes. Specifically, we are talking about adult-onset type 2 diabetes. While some people are genetically predisposed to develop it, this is basically a lifestyle disease. It's the most serious chronic disease you can get because it causes multiple health problems. Diabetes raises the risk of heart disease, cancer, blindness, kidney failure, and limb amputation drastically. If nobody had diabetes our society would be far healthier!

Some have described the rise in cases of diabetes as a *pandemic*, which means a disease which has become prevalent worldwide. While it's estimated that nearly 500 million people have diabetes globally, it's most prevalent in affluent, developed societies like the United States. The primary culprits are weight gain and an increasingly sedentary lifestyle. People living in rural areas tend to have much lower rates of diabetes despite stereotypes – and the reason is they are more physically active throughout the day.

So what causes diabetes? To find out, let's learn a little about what happens when you eat something. This isn't a science book so our discussion will be casual.

First, let's look at the 4 types of "macronutrients" in your diet:

- Fat
- Carbohydrates
- Protein
- Fiber

"Fiber" provides bulk and not much else, so technically it's not really a "macronutrient", but it's a major part of many foods so we're listing it here. You're not going to digest it and get calories or gain weight. In the case of diabetes, fat and protein aren't relevant so let's have a look at how carbs are digested.

Sugar is the most basic carbohydrate. There are more complex carbohydrates, such as starches and "complex carbohydrates" that are basically long chains of sugars. When you eat sugar, it does into your bloodstream and the body then reacts to make use of it, by releasing the hormone *insulin* from your pancreas.

When it comes to sugar, insulin has two basic functions:

- It encourages cells to take up the sugar, which they can use for energy.
- It causes excess calories or sugar consumed to be converted into body fat.

When we're young, this process works well for most of us. However, over time the body gets used to the insulin. What happens when you become desensitized to something? It doesn't work as well. The first time you see a horror movie or rode a roller coaster maybe it scared you out of your wits, right? But the second and third time it becomes less and less scary.

The same thing happens with insulin. Over time, in many people, the cells begin to respond to insulin less and less. The person is becoming *insulin resistant*. So the pancreas responds by releasing more insulin to get the job done. We can measure the effectiveness of this system by looking at fasting blood sugar, which is your blood sugar reading after you have gone about 10-12 hours without eating anything.

Since the cells aren't taking up sugar from the blood as well as they used to, blood sugar rises. A normal person has a fasting blood sugar level of 100 mg/dL or less. People who are developing diabetes but not yet diabetic will have fasting blood sugar ranging from more than 100 mg/dL up to around 125 mg/dL. If it's higher than 125 mg/dL, most doctors will give a diagnosis of type 2 diabetes.

For someone who is "normal", a meal of carbohydrates won't raise blood sugar too much, but it's considered acceptable if your blood sugar peaks at about 140 mg/dL about 1-2 hours after eating. If someone has pre-diabetes or outright type 2 diabetes, blood sugar after a meal of carbs can rise to 180 mg/dL or higher.

These kinds of *blood sugar spikes* cause major damage to the body. In particular, they cause damage to blood vessels. At first, small blood vessels and capillaries are damaged, and this can lead to erectile dysfunction, kidney disease, and even blindness. Wounds don't heal normally because they don't get proper blood flow, and if left untreated people with this type of blood vessel damage can get severe infections requiring amputation.

Over time, the larger arteries are also damaged. Diabetics are at higher risk of a heart attack or stroke, and diabetics tend to have heart attacks and strokes at younger ages than the general population.

And that's not all. Diabetics are also at increased risk for developing major cancers. It turns out that cancer cells thrive in a high sugar environment. So while the rest of your body is struggling with high blood sugars, and cancer cells that are around are loving it and thriving. In fact, research has shown that administering the diabetes blood sugar controlling drug *metformin* significantly reduces cancer risk.

Besides causing all these problems since insulin isn't working so well diabetics tend to gain weight. All-in-all, this is a health problem you want to avoid.

We might focus for a minute on so-called pre-diabetes. This is often associated with a health problem that used to be thought of as a normal consequence of entering "middle age".

You might notice that people in their 40s and 50s suddenly start getting pot belly's, or fat around the mid-section. They will probably develop other problems too. For starters, their blood sugars will enter the pre-diabetes range. They also have high blood pressure, and blood tests will probably show problems with their blood lipids.

The blood lipids (lipid = fat) your doctor will measure include:

- Total cholesterol
- LDL or low-density "bad" cholesterol
- HDL or high-density "good" cholesterol
- Triglycerides

LDL is called "bad" cholesterol because it can stick to the artery walls and eventually cause heart disease. HDL acts as a cleanup man in the bloodstream, it transports excess LDL back to the liver, and it also tries to clean up LDL from your artery walls.

If you have high LDL cholesterol, you're at increased risk of heart attack or stroke. If you have high HDL, you're at lower risk of heart attack or stroke. Many doctors actually measure the HDL to LDL ratio to get a risk measure for heart disease.

Triglycerides, until recently, have not been considered all that important. It turns out that high triglycerides are directly linked to the risk caused by LDL cholesterol and the level of HDL cholesterol.

When you have high triglycerides, your LDL cholesterol becomes smaller and denser. This makes it more likely to stick to your artery walls. Triglycerides are also associated with low HDL levels, although the reason isn't quite clear. They are also associated with high blood sugars.

So one way to look at a person with metabolic syndrome is that besides being overweight in the midsection, high blood sugars and high blood pressure, they will have high triglycerides and low HDL as well.

That's why the guy with the fat stomach in his 40s or 50s is a heart attack waiting to happen and if that doesn't get him or her at a young age, they're on the fast track toward developing diabetes.

Previously, it was thought (and still is in some circles) that high triglycerides were related to fat consumption. In fact, high triglycerides are related to high sugar consumption (sugar in the general sense – any carbohydrate). People on the keto diet, for example, who eat very low carb, usually see their triglyceride levels drop.

However there is another way to drop your triglycerides, and it's by consuming fish oil. The fattier fish you eat the more your triglycerides will drop.

## Heart Health and You

A solid measurement of risk for heart disease is to take your fasting triglyceride number and divide it by your fasting HDL number. If it's greater than 2.5, your heart disease risk is elevated. If it's less than 2.5, you're at low risk of heart disease and the lower the number the better.

For example, consider a hypothetical patient named Martha. Her HDL level is 50 mg/dL and her fasting triglycerides are 120 mg/dL. Her triglyceride to HDL ratio is:

Martha's ratio = 120/50 = 2.4

Martha is at moderately low risk for heart disease. She'd be a little better off lowering her triglyceride level a little bit and she probably needs to exercise a little more.

Martha's friend Sally has a fasting HDL of 35 and a fasting triglyceride level of 250. Her ratio is:

Sally = 250/35 = 7.14

Sally has an extremely high triglyceride to HDL level (> 5). Sally is at high risk of heart attack over the next five to ten years. Sally also has high blood sugars, her fasting level ranges between 110 mg/dL and 120 mg/dL, making her pre-diabetic. Sally needs to make major lifestyle changes.

On the other hand, Martha's friend Bob, who eats fish daily and exercises, has a fasting triglyceride level of 70 and an HDL level of 55.

His ratio is:

Bob = 70/55 = 1.3

When it comes to heart disease, Bob is by far the healthiest. It's probably pretty likely he has very little chance of a heart attack in the next ten years provided he maintains his healthy lifestyle.

It turns out you can adopt Bob's heart-healthy lifestyle and reduce your own risk factors! This can be done by adopting the DASH-Mediterranean solution. By increasing your fish and keeping your blood sugars in control you can go a long way towards managing your triglycerides. This is something that the DASH diet taken alone does not do.

HDL is a tougher nut to crack. While some people see HDL levels respond to dietary changes, others do not. Attempts to develop pharmaceuticals to raise triglycerides have failed so far. Some people may see HDL levels improve with vigorous exercise and weight loss. However, you can still greatly improve your risk factors simply by lowering triglycerides even if your HDL levels don't change.

Now a note about saturated fat. When you eat saturated fat, your liver makes more LDL cholesterol. Despite its connotation as "bad", your body needs some LDL cholesterol. What LDL does is transport cholesterol to the cells and organs throughout the body where it's needed to carry out the basic functions of life. In fact, people with very low cholesterol (total cholesterol of 160 or lower) are actually at higher risk for many diseases and have been shown to have shorter lifespans on average.

But while low cholesterol is bad, too much is bad too. The more LDL cholesterol you have in your bloodstream the higher the chance that it will stick to your arteries and lead to heart attack and stroke. And it's a basic fact – the more saturated fat you eat per day the more LDL cholesterol you're going to have. In fact, one dietary strategy you can employ to lower your cholesterol is to simply limit your daily consumption of saturated fat to 20 g per day or less.

However, as time has gone on the picture of health we have has become more complicated. As mentioned earlier, if you're eating saturated fat but have a lower carbohydrate intake (especially simple carbs like sugar and starch), your LDL particles tend to be larger and less damaging. Larger

LDL particles are less likely to stick to artery walls. This phenomenon is associated with triglyceride levels, lower triglycerides correlate with bigger and safer LDL particles. So eating saturated fat *by itself* is not a risk factor to be concerned about – you need to look at it within the context of your overall diet and lipid profile. You can even find out by getting a blood test that will measure the concentration of small, dense LDL particles in your blood, but that is often something you have to request from your doctor, and not usually part of a standard cholesterol test.

## *Real Foods and Processed Foods*

Earlier we noted that fast food and junk food have become prominent in the American diet over the past 5-7 decades. These foods have become known as *processed* foods. There are several ways that processed foods can impact health, including:

- Processed foods often include simple carbohydrates. When it comes to a plant like wheat, you're actually eating the seed of the plant. It has three parts including the "germ", which is the embryo of a new plant if you were to plant the seed, an outer shell called bran, and the starchy part of the seed where all the calories are. If you ate the entire seed, it would take some effort by your body to break it down and digest the starch. That leads to a slower rise in blood sugars, helping you avoid dangerous spikes. Foods that include the entire seed are known as *whole grains*. On the other hand, if you refine the grain and only include the starchy part, you have a processed food like white flour. Since the starch has been extracted by itself, it digests rapidly and leads to blood sugar spikes. Factory made processed foods are often made from refined flour. For extreme examples, think of white bread and cake.

- Processed foods are often high in salt. While there are some good whole grain snack foods, they also tend to be high in salt. While some people are more sensitive than others, high salt foods can increase blood pressure endangering health.
- Many processed foods combine starch, oils, and salt together in one package, creating a tasty snack that raises your blood sugar *and* your blood pressure. French fries and potato chips are the best examples.
- Processed meats are high in salt and many are high in nitrates. The high salt content can raise your blood

pressure if processed meats are consumed on a regular basis. While the link isn't quite certain, eating a lot of nitrate and nitrite-containing foods may raise the risk of certain cancers.

You can see that eating processed foods isn't the best thing for your health. You're far better off eating natural, whole food diet. The Mediterranean diet has this feature "built-in". Emphasizing whole grains, lean meat and fish, and lots of fruits and vegetables, the Mediterranean diet will help you reach your health goals which can include healthier blood sugars and triglyceride levels.

With its low sodium approach and also including wholesome, real foods, the DASH diet helps meet blood pressure goals.

In this chapter, we've discussed the problems of high blood pressure, diabetes, and heart disease and nutritional factors that can increase your risk. In the next chapter, we'll look specifically at the DASH diet.

# Chapter 2: Intro to the DASH DIET

The health problems seen in the last chapter are related to two things – what you're eating and how much you weigh. If you're not obese, you can still have major health problems like high blood pressure and not even know it. In this chapter, we're going to explain what the DASH diet is and how it works.

### *What is DASH?*

The DASH diet was developed to treat high blood pressure using natural methods. This isn't going to work for all people, some people simply need medications because of family history/genetic reasons. However it's going to have some impact and might prevent you from developing high blood pressure and for those who already have it, it may reduce their blood pressure and reduce the need for medications.

The main principle behind the DASH diet is focusing on sodium. Dietary factors have a large influence on blood pressure (as does obesity). Specifically, there are a few minerals that influence fluid levels and the relaxation or contraction of your blood vessels.

These are:

- Sodium – found in table salt and MSG, and also a natural part of nearly every food including meats. Sodium causes fluid retention and promotes blood vessel contraction.
- Potassium – found in leafy green vegetables, nuts, and avocados, and in lesser amounts in meats. Potassium discourages fluid retention and promotes blood vessel relaxation. Also found in high quantities in many fruits like oranges, apples, and bananas.
- Magnesium – found in nuts, vegetables, and avocados. Magnesium helps relax the heart and blood vessels and stabilizes heart rhythms, and promotes regular digestion.
- Calcium – found in dairy products and leafy green vegetables. Helps promote blood vessel relaxation. Most people are also aware that adequate calcium intake is necessary for strong bones and warding off osteoporosis.

The fact is your body needs all these minerals. So it's not fair to think of salt as "bad", without adequate salt you would die. The problem is Americans consume way too much salt. It's estimated that a reasonable daily intake of sodium is about 2,400 mg per day. The average American consumes about 3,500 mg per day.

Many if not most Americans are also deficient in potassium and magnesium. What this means is that people are *out of balance* when it comes to the minerals they need to keep their cardiovascular system operating in an optimal fashion. The strategy behind the DASH diet is to bring nutrition into a balance, and so help with blood pressure.

Let's quickly understand how blood pressure works. Pressure and a pump of some kind is necessary to distribute fluids. If you have a given amount of water and force it through a narrow pipe, the pressure will be higher than if you pump the same amount of water through a larger pipe.

Your heart and circulatory system work the same way, with your heart acting as the pump and your arteries playing the role of the pipes in the water system. However, unlike most pipes constructed to transport water, your blood vessels are flexible and can tighten or relax. When they tighten, your blood pressure goes up. Blood pressure is measured in "millimeters of mercury", or mm Hg, because historically pressures were measured by seeing how much pressure raised a column of mercury in a narrow glass tube as it was increased.

BP or Blood Pressure is a ratio between systolic/diastolic blood pressure. Systolic blood pressure tells you what the pressure in your arteries is when the heart pumps (when it's forcing blood into the arteries). Diastolic blood pressure tells you what the pressure is when the heart is relaxed (so no new blood is being forced into the arteries). Most doctors consider 120/80 or lower to be a healthy blood pressure.

This can cause a lot of problems. It weakens and stiffens the arteries, which can cause them to burst over time. It also damages them in such a way that makes the buildup of arterial plaque more likely, raising the chances of heart disease (and a reason why having high blood pressure *and* high LDL cholesterol sets up a dangerous situation).

Excess potassium, calcium, or magnesium can disrupt the circulatory system as well, causing heart rhythm disturbances. If they get bad enough, it can even be life-threatening.

If you're not a health scientist, you don't need to know the nitty-gritty details. Just remember that:

- Excess salt means higher blood pressure.
- Salt (sodium) is not evil – you need salt as much as you need many other nutrients but at the right amount.
- Our food industry has gone overboard with salt. It's a cheap, easy way to flavor food. But they've created a situation where there is excess salt in the diets of most people.
- Excess potassium, calcium or magnesium can cause problems too. However, this isn't a problem for most people, since most Americans actually have deficiencies in these minerals.
- Balance is what we're after – for health you need to balance sodium, potassium, magnesium, and calcium.

Now that we know the rationale behind the DASH diet, let's look at the actual content of the DASH diet.

The DASH diet consists of the following rules, based on a typical 2,000 calorie per day diet:

- Eat large amounts of fruits and vegetables, 8-10 servings per day. Typically you should consume 4-5 servings of fruit and vegetables. When consuming whole fruit, one medium fruit (an apple, orange, kiwi, etc.) is a single serving. On a per cup basis, the ½ cup is a serving. This rule applies for fresh, canned, dried, or frozen fruit. For fruit juice, since the fiber has been removed and there is relatively higher sugar content, ¼ of a cup constitutes one serving. For vegetables, a half cup of most vegetables is a serving but for lettuce 1 cup is allowed.
- Whole grains – eat 7-8 servings per day. Consumption of simple or refined carbs is not allowed, so no white flour or white rice. Look for the phrase whole grain on the label of any bread, pasta, or cereal. Serving size is a ½ cup and for bread 1 slice.
- Dairy – 2-3 servings per day. The DASH diet recommends low-fat dairy products in moderation. For milk or yogurt, one cup is a serving. For cheese one serving is an ounce and a half. Frozen yogurt and ice cream are not recommended, as they are

considered sweets which are consumed in strict moderation.

- Meats are consumed in moderation. The DASH diet recommends that you consume 1-2 servings of lean meats per day or even no meat in a given day. This should include skinless poultry, seafood, and fish. Beef and pork are allowed but only lean cuts consumed now and then. On a meatless day, you can substitute beans or legumes for protein.

- Beans, nuts, and seeds – consumed in moderation. Limit to one serving per day of beans OR nuts OR seeds. One serving is a ½ cup of beans, 1/3 cup of nuts, or two tbsp. of seeds.

- Oil, salad dressing, and fat-containing condiments like mayo, 2-3 servings per day – consumed in strict moderation. The diet allows 2 tbsp. of low-fat salad dressing or 1 tbsp. of low-fat mayo. One tsp. of oil or "soft margarine" is considered one serving.

- Sweets – consume up to five times per week. On the DASH diet, the definition of "sweets" is limited, including yogurt with fruit (1 cup per serving), frozen yogurt, and low fat or fat-free ice cream (1/2 cup per serving). Also included here are modest amounts of jam, syrup, honey, and sugar, with a serving size of one tbsp..

- Careful with added salt: Generally, you're discouraged from adding salt to your foods, especially when eating out. If you utilize soy sauce or salt-laden sauces such as teriyaki opt for low-sodium varieties.

Eggs are not specifically mentioned in most guides for the DASH diet; however, you're allowed 4 eggs per week and can also have 2 additional servings of egg whites.

There is a version of the DASH diet known as the BOLD diet. The BOLD diet follows the same rules as the DASH diet, but it allows you to consume lean beef. So if you wanted to, your 1-2 servings of meat could contain lean beef whenever you wanted it. Studies of the BOLD diet have shown it works as well as the DASH diet, even showing some benefits to blood lipids.

The DASH diet is quite restrictive in many respects. It was based on what was thought to be true about diet in the early 1990s – that fat was bad. The Mediterranean diet takes a different view on that, so is more flexible and tolerable than what's presented here.

That said – the DASH diet does lead to weight loss and works very well when reducing blood pressure. On average, the DASH diet has been found to lower blood pressure.

## *Who is the DASH diet for?*

The real answer is the DASH diet is for anyone who wants to live a healthy lifestyle. The DASH diet is not a calorie counting diet, but it limits the overall calorie intake by having you follow pre-determined portion sizes and amounts while also emphasizing nutrient dense but calorie light foods. Many foods on the DASH food list have high fiber content. This helps aid regular digestion but also makes you feel full or satiated sooner. As a result of this alone, you're more likely to consume fewer calories. This can help with weight loss.

In short, the DASH diet is for:

- Anyone with high blood pressure, or questionable blood pressure.
- Anyone with a family history of issues with blood pressure, even if they don't have high blood pressure themselves.

- Anyone with pre-diabetes or who is diagnosed as a type 2 diabetic.
- Anyone who is overweight and needs an easy-to-follow system to promote weight loss.
- Anyone who simply wants a lifelong program that promotes healthy eating.

While in some ways the DASH diet is pretty strict, one of the benefits of the DASH diet is that it doesn't prohibit any food outright. So while you should observe the guidelines most of the time, the occasional steak, chicken wings, or piece of cake is not going to throw your body into chaos and destroy the diet. This contrasts with many radical diets like Atkins that prohibit entire food groups. Since Atkins depends on "ketosis" (burning fat for energy rather than glucose), one simple cheating episode can completely destroy it (by kicking you out of ketosis). The DASH diet doesn't suffer from this problem.

Also, since the DASH diet is really a healthier version of simply consuming all food groups, it fits in easier with eating out and dealing with social situations than many other diets do. The DASH diet can also be readily adapted to vegetarian and even vegan diets, just by substituting beans and legumes for meats and using dairy substitutes.

## *Health Benefits of the DASH Diet*

If you've been eating a standard American diet, that is high in carbs, high in fat, high in sugar, and high in salt while low in vital nutrients like potassium and magnesium, the DASH diet is going to amount to a major reset. The health benefits of the DASH diet are broad-based.

- Keeps your blood pressure in check. This will lower your heart related diseases, stroke, brain hemorrhage, and kidney issues.
- Helps you lose weight and maintain weight loss. The DASH diet will generate steady, long-term weight loss. While some diets like ketogenic or Atkins may generate a lot of weight loss in the first couple of weeks, following an eating plan like DASH will lead to more sustainable weight loss over time, even though it starts out slow.
- By assisting with weight loss, it will reduce obesity.
- By keeping your weight in check, it reduces the risk for many cancers.

- DASH helps maintain healthy blood sugars and reduces insulin resistance by emphasizing wholesome, natural high-fiber foods.
- DASH will keep your LDL cholesterol in check, reducing the risk of heart disease.
- DASH will help prevent and even reverse pre-diabetes and can help control type 2 diabetes.
- By reducing blood sugar spikes, it will help improve mood and energy levels.
- Some claim DASH even makes people look and feel younger.

## *Sodium*

The DASH diets central focus is on sodium. It's not a no-salt diet, even though it's developed a reputation for this over the years. Remember the average American consumes about 3,500 mg of sodium per day (and even more for a lot of folks). The DASH diet brings sodium consumption down to more reasonable levels:

- The Standard DASH diet limits daily sodium intake to 2,300 mg per day.
- The low-sodium DASH diet limits daily sodium intake to 1,500 mg per day. This is recommended for people

over 50, and those already diagnosed with prehypertension and those with high blood pressure.

## The Science Behind the Dash Diet

Scientific studies have estimated that if everyone with high blood pressure adhered to the DASH diet, the number of heart attacks, strokes, and hemorrhages over a ten year period could be reduced by 400,000 in the United States alone!

While the DASH diet leads to slow and steady weight loss, it shows results quickly when it comes to blood pressure. Many see results in as few as two weeks. It shows the most impact in people who are older and/or already have high blood pressure. DASH also reduces blood pressure in people who have only mildly elevated blood pressure, a level at which your doctor is likely to advise "lifestyle" changes rather than put you on prescription medication.

## The history behind the DASH Diet

Medical professionals began recognizing the link between high blood pressure and diseases of the kidney and heart in the 19th century. At first, this link was only recognized with the kidneys but later doctors began to see that high blood pressure could cause heart problems even without kidney damage. Cuff-based blood pressure measurements were developed at the very end of the 19<sup>th</sup> century allowing nurses and doctors to actually measure blood pressure in clinics.

Despite some awareness of the relation between blood pressure and health issues, blood pressure in and of itself wasn't recognized as a health problem until much later. In fact, even up into the 1950s doctors referred to blood pressure up to 210/100 as "benign blood pressure". This is seen as absurd now, and blood pressure of 210/100 would be considered a medical emergency.

In the late 1930s, the first dietary approach to reducing blood pressure was developed. It was coined the "rice diet", which actually required hospitalization in its early phases. It got the name rice diet because plain white rice was the primary component of the diet, which also included fruit, fruit juices, and sugar. Sodium was limited to 250 mg per day. If this was successful then lean meats and vegetables were added to the diet.

Today, we know that limiting salt intake to 250 mg per day is not healthy and in fact dangerous, even if doing so would drop blood pressure. The first pharmaceutical treatments that were actually effective and well tolerated were diuretic medications, which became available in the late 1950s. These drugs were designed to remove excess sodium and fluid from the body. By reducing fluid, lowering blood pressure is possible. Unfortunately, diuretics also remove other vital nutrients like potassium from the body, and they work mainly by increasing the amount of urination.

In the following two decades, many other medications, starting with beta blockers, were developed that lowered blood pressure far more effectively with fewer of the undesirable results seen with previous methods. Other research was pointing toward dietary intervention, showing that consumption of certain minerals and high fiber in the diet would lead to reductions in blood pressure.

In 1992, the National Heart, Lung, and Blood Institute, a part of the National Institutes of Health in the United States, set out to design a diet that would help reduce and control high blood pressure, but one that was not as draconian as the rice diet. The goal was to develop a balanced diet that utilized all food groups and ensured that the participant got adequate levels of sodium in balance with potassium, magnesium, and calcium. Food that was conventionally eaten already by the general public was chosen for the diet. The idea being that it would be easy for the general public to adopt the diet. Actual trials began in 1993 and lasted until around 1997.

As we've seen the research trials found that the DASH diet showed significant reductions in blood pressure values. Since the idea behind the DASH diet was to increase consumption of potassium, magnesium, and calcium, during the study it was compared to a diet that let people eat what they wanted, but increased their consumption of fruits and vegetables. This diet did show benefits when it comes to blood pressure, with modest improvements. However what we know as the standard DASH diet today proved more effective, while also encouraging weight loss.

The trials conclusively demonstrated that the DASH diet reduces and controls high blood pressure effectively. Later studies showed that control of sodium intake alone had a major impact on blood pressure, but that doing that with a DASH diet had the most impact. Since the late 1990s, the role of sodium by itself in elevated blood pressure has come into question. It's still generally accepted that high sodium intake will raise blood pressure, however, some people are more sensitive to this than others and most people don't consume enough sodium for it to be very significant. The real culprit appears to be a diet lacking in proper levels of magnesium and potassium.

The health benefits of the DASH diet are clear, but what if we could make them even better? It turns out you can, and one way is to incorporate the principles of the Mediterranean diet. If you looked at a "food pyramid" of the two diets, you'd see that they are fairly similar. So integrating a Mediterranean lifestyle with the DASH diet can be done relatively easily. But before we get into that we'll have to learn about the Mediterranean diet in its own right. This is the topic of the next chapter.

# Chapter 3: An Overview of the Mediterranean Diet

Now we turn our attention to the famed Mediterranean diet. As the name implies this diet is based on foods eaten in the Mediterranean region. To see why this might be relevant, we visited the website *worldlifeexpectancy.com*, which collects data on death rates from a multitude of causes from the World Health Organization, or WHO.

https://www.worldlifeexpectancy.com/cause-of-death/coronary-heart-disease/by-country/

The death rate per 100,000 people from coronary heart disease in the United States is 86.89. However, looking at the death rates in some Mediterranean countries reveals some startling numbers:

- Portugal: 47.23
- Spain: 49.62
- France: 43.25
- Italy: 64.95

Another way to look at it is Portugal has a 46% reduction in coronary heart disease deaths as compared to the United States. For Spain, France, and Italy the reduction is 43%, 50%, and 25% respectively. While some of the reduction could be due to factors such as genetics and the healthcare systems in each country, these are quite dramatic numbers. And this is using recent data from 2018, a time when historical traditions aren't as closely followed as they used to be.

There is no question that the numbers shown here are due in large part to diet, and the historical evidence that this is so is even stronger. Researchers began noticing that after the second world war, the incidence of many chronic western diseases was found to be lower in the Mediterranean countries than it was in other countries like the United States. At that time, researchers didn't know much about omega-3 fatty acids, or even about the benefits of eating whole grain foods and fruits and vegetables. However, as new knowledge developed, it became apparent that the foods consumed in the traditional Mediterranean diet were having a major impact on the incidence of heart attack, stroke, and cancer in these countries. Unfortunately in recent years with the spread of globalization and

American fast food, traditional ways of living are being abandoned and some of these countries, Greece in particular, are seeing a substantial rise in heart disease-related illness and death.

So what kind of foods are consumed in a traditional Mediterranean diet? We're going to see that it's not substantially different than the DASH diet, but it does have some major differences. In particular, consuming a lot more fat is an important part of the Mediterranean diet – the key is to consume the right kinds of fat. Also, drinking wine is important – or at least allowed- part of the diet.

## What is the Mediterranean Diet

When you think of the Mediterranean and food, as an American you're probably having visions of pizza and spaghetti. This flawed view is a result of the popularized version of Italian-American culture. The reality of traditional Mediterranean cuisine is quite different, and it has ancient roots going back to the Roman Empire and beyond.

The Mediterranean diet arose quite naturally. In other words, people living in the mostly moderate climate of the

Mediterranean either right on the sea or close to it simply ate the kinds of foods that were available in the region. Three foods come to mind:

- Fish
- Olives
- Grapes

The mild climate of the region created conditions that were favorable for the growth of olive trees and grapes. As a result, people quickly learned how to make olive oil and wine. Red wine, in particular, has been popular in the region for centuries if not eons. Olive oil and red wine are frequently mentioned in the Bible and other ancient writings from the region. Romans were known for their indulgence in red wine (at least rich Romans) and Greeks enjoyed it as well. The abundance of fish in the Mediterranean sea and nearby eastern Atlantic also helped drive the adaptation of fish as a major protein source. The region is also favorable for many nuts. While nuts and fish might be viewed as luxuries on the DASH diet, they play a more central role in the Mediterranean diet.

Like we did for the DASH diet, we can imagine a Mediterranean version of the so-called food pyramid. While there are some similarities, there are also a lot of differences.

- The Mediterranean diet emphasizes the consumption of fruits and vegetables in large amounts. This includes many of the same fruits and vegetables that are found on the DASH diet, such as oranges, apples, spinach, kale, carrots, and arugula. However, on a Mediterranean diet liberal consumption of avocadoes is encouraged, rather than limited.
- Whole grains are an important part of the Mediterranean diet, including whole grain bread, brown and wild rice, whole grain pasta, couscous, and grains like quinoa.
- Cheese and yogurt can form part of a Mediterranean diet, but these dairy items are not consumed on a daily basis.
- Beans, olive oil, nuts, seeds, and legumes are consumed liberally on a Mediterranean diet.
- Fish and seafood are highly encouraged. Many people living on the coast eat fish and seafood all the time, on

a Mediterranean diet you should eat fish at least twice per week.

- Eggs and Poultry are consumed in moderation, but not on a daily basis.
- Less frequently consumed items include red meat (beef and lamb), pork, and sweets.

Now that we have a general idea of what kinds of foods are included on a Mediterranean diet, let's look at some of the major differences between the Mediterranean diet and the DASH diet.

- The DASH diet limits you to one serving per day of beans, or nuts, or seeds. The Mediterranean diet encourages you to consume these items daily and places no limits on their consumption.
- The DASH diet limits you to low-fat dairy. While dairy is consumed in moderation on the Mediterranean diet, there are no limitations specified as to fat content.
- The DASH diet specifies the servings of fruits and vegetables per day. The Mediterranean diet places no limits.

- The DASH diet is a low-fat diet. The Mediterranean diet is a high-fat diet, but it stresses the consumption of healthy fats. These include monounsaturated fats found in olive and avocados, as well as omega-3 fats found in fatty fish.

- Since the DASH diet is a low-fat diet, it places restrictions on the amounts of condiments like mayo and salad dressing that can be consumed. The Mediterranean diet places no limits on these items provided that the fat they contain comes from healthy monounsaturated fats. So for example, an olive oil based mayo is perfectly acceptable on a Mediterranean diet. An olive oil and vinegar salad dressing would be acceptable as well, however, a ranch dressing that uses a soybean oil base would be discouraged.

- While the consumption of alcohol isn't strictly prohibited on the DASH diet, it's discouraged because of the impact on blood pressure (for some people, and depending on the amount consumed). In contrast, red wine can be consumed on the Mediterranean diet, and in fact, 1-2 drinks daily is encouraged. Of course, if you have an alcohol problem or don't drink at all, don't use the diet as an excuse to take up regular drinking.

- Throughout all the food groups, the DASH diet has specific portion sizes and rules on the number of portions consumed per day. The approach with the Mediterranean diet is different. There are no rules on portions or portion sizes. The rule for the Mediterranean diet is more basic – eat until you're satisfied and no more. For many people, this makes the diet feel more flexible and easier to follow.

While these differences seem substantial, we'll see they aren't as big as they seem at first meets the eye, and it's relatively easy to incorporate Mediterranean style eating into the DASH diet.

## Health Benefits of the Mediterranean Diet

We've already touched on the issue of health, noting that in the Mediterranean region, especially when adherence to traditional diets was widespread, the levels of chronic diseases were lower than in the United States, and still are in many cases. This is especially true when it comes to heart disease.

We've already mentioned that a scientist named Alan Keys discovered there was a relationship between cholesterol and heart disease. While we now know that the relationship is far more complicated than he imagined, and unfortunately his research results were misinterpreted to mean that people should follow strict low-fat diets, he also made some important observations about the Mediterranean countries.

Immediately after the war, Keys noted that people in war-torn areas of Italy and Greece seemed to be in pretty good health. At first, it was thought that obesity was rare because of the war, but it turns out that obesity was actually rare because of the diet most people were consuming at the time. There was also a documented lack of chronic "western" diseases.

Studies have compared following a high-fat Mediterranean diet with a traditional low-fat diet which is advised after a heart attack. It's been found that the Mediterranean diet rich in fat from seafood, olive oil, and nuts reduces the risk of a second heart attack by up to 70% as compared to following the traditional low-fat diet advocated by the American Heart Association and others.

Studies have also shown that following a Mediterranean diet reduces the risk of a heart attack at a level similar to that obtained by taking statin drugs.

## Regular intake of Fruits and Vegetables lessens the chances of many diseases

We've already noted that fruits and vegetables help supply the body with vital potassium and magnesium. And in the case of leafy green vegetables, they also help supply calcium as well. These minerals help balance out the electrolytes in your body that control blood pressure and heart rhythm and keep muscles healthy as well. If you're getting a lot of muscle cramps you might want to look at your consumption of potassium and magnesium.

However, the benefits of fruits and vegetables don't end there. Certainly, you're aware that they are packed with vitamins that are needed for health including vitamins A & C that will help you maintain a healthy immune system. Leafy green vegetables also contain vitamin K. There are two types of vitamin K, K1 is important for proper blood clotting, and K2 helps keep your arteries clear of calcium, which promotes heart health.

Fruits and vegetables also provide a large amount of dietary fiber. This helps keep your digestion regular, and it also helps you to maintain a healthy gut biome. Remember that your stomach and intestines are home for a large population of bacteria, most of which exist with us in a symbiotic relationship. These bacteria help digest your food, and keeping the right balance of healthy bacteria is important for health. One way to do this is by supplying them with the fibers contained in many fruits and vegetables.

Fruits and vegetables also provide many micronutrients, antioxidants, and so-called phytonutrients which can help reduce the risk of cancer.

In fact, leafy green vegetables play an important role in digestive health related to colon cancer. It's been found that in the absence of leafy greens, consuming red meat can cause the formation of certain cancer-causing substances in the colon that promote colon cancer. Eating red meat alone might cause benign polyps to turn into aggressive cancers. These substances are actually created by the bacteria in your intestines.

However, if you eat your steak with leafy green vegetables, this doesn't happen. The digestion of the leafy greens keeps the bacteria occupied and the cancer-causing substances they make during the digestion of red meat by itself aren't made. You might file this away in the steak + baked potato = bad and the steak + leafy greens = good files.

## Health benefits of whole grains

Whole grain foods, as we've discussed before, provide a healthier way to get carbohydrates. Let's review – if you eat a meal high in sugar, you're going to get a blood sugar spike. The simpler the carbohydrates in the food you eat, the faster they're digested and the higher your blood sugar spike. Blood sugar spikes are bad for you, causing damage throughout the circulatory system.

Whole grain foods minimize blood sugar spikes. Simply put, it takes longer to break them down, so you'll get a longer but shallower and smoother rise in blood sugar. That's far healthier.

Whole grain foods also provide a lot of important vitamins and minerals. For example, whole grain pasta made from wheat berries contains thiamin, niacin, riboflavin, B6, phosphorous, zinc, iron, magnesium, manganese, and potassium. In addition, it's rich in fiber.

To summarize, whole grain bread, pasta, and grains provide vitamins, minerals, and fiber, while providing liberal energy from carbohydrates without the blood sugar spikes.

## Health benefits of olive oil

Olive oil might be considered as a magical elixir. While you probably don't want to drink a large glass and should watch it since fat packs a lot of calories in smaller amounts, it's definitely something you want to use liberally, rather than sparingly in your diet.

In fact, olive oil based diets have been directly compared to low-fat diets in large scientific studies. It's been demonstrated that following a Mediterranean style diet that uses liberal amounts of olive oil reduces the risk of contracting diabetes by 50% when compared to following a low-fat diet. The documented decrease in the risk of diabetes was found to be independent of other factors, like obesity at the beginning of the study or level of physical activity.

Studies in Europe have shown that liberal olive oil use helps reduce the incidence of stroke. In fact, one study found that people who used olive oil daily and in large amounts reduced their risk of stroke by up to 40%. Again, this reduction in risk was found to be independent of other factors like exercise level or body weight.

Olive oil also improves arterial function. As we age, our arteries don't work as well as they used to. They become stiffened and less responsive. Think of them as old pipes. However, researchers have found that olive oil helps to keep the arteries young and supple.

Another area where liberal use of olive oil helps is in preventing or even reversing metabolic syndrome. Remember that metabolic syndrome is characterized by a fat stomach or midsection. Inside the body, people with metabolic syndrome have high blood sugar, high blood sugar, high levels of bad LDL cholesterol and triglycerides, and low HDL or "good" cholesterol. Large studies have shown that liberal use of olive oil can have moderate but significant effects in reducing the waistline, reducing blood pressure, reducing bad cholesterol, reducing triglycerides, and raising HDL cholesterol. This was modest but independent of other factors. In other words, it can help a person overcome metabolic syndrome when used in combination with other lifestyle changes.

Olive oil may also protect against the development of certain cancers. Olive oil contains a phytonutrient named *oleocanthal*, which helps reduce inflammation in the body. By reducing inflammation, it helps reduce the risk of certain cancers including breast and prostate cancer. Inflammation is also an important factor in the development of heart disease, by the way.

Olive oil contains many fats of all types, including 11% saturated fat. However, it's about 73% monounsaturated fat. Monounsaturated fats have been shown to reduce bad cholesterol and lower triglycerides – so consumption of liberal amounts of monounsaturated fats like olive oil can significantly lessen the chances of a heart attack and stroke. Monounsaturated fats also slightly lower blood pressure. They also reduce insulin resistance (see chapter one), making the body more efficient when processing carbohydrates.

An inflammatory marker that is associated with elevated heart attack risk is called C - reactive protein, or CRP. It's been found that consuming a diet rich in olive oil can reduce CRP by about 15%. And the more olive oil consumed, the more CRP was reduced. By reducing the level of inflammation, you can reduce the chance of sudden death from a heart attack.

Olive oil also supplies some important vitamins – specifically it provides vitamins E and K.

Experts recommend consuming extra-virgin olive oil.

## Health benefits of consuming fatty fish

Fatty fish is consumed throughout the Mediterranean region, where sardines, mackerel, tuna, and swordfish are very popular. In addition, people consume a large number of anchovies.

Eating fatty fish has two benefits. By eating fish rather than beef, you're reducing the amount of saturated fat in the diet. Remember that while saturated fat in and of itself isn't necessarily bad, it does raise LDL cholesterol. All else being equal, that's not a good thing (although as we discussed in the previous chapter, the effect can be harmless if your triglycerides are low).

The main benefit of eating fish, however, is that fatty fish supplies the body with omega-3 fatty acids. Omega-3 fats have several health benefits.

- They stabilize heart rhythms.
- They reduce inflammation.
- They reduce triglycerides.

Overall, people who consume fatty fish in large amounts have far lower rates of heart disease and stroke. People expected that they could duplicate these benefits by packaging fish oil in pills, but that hasn't turned out to be as fruitful as people originally hoped. It may be that the omega-3 oils in pills could reduce the incidence of heart disease but they aren't given in the correct dosages. In any case, eating fatty fish at least twice a week has been conclusively demonstrated significantly lessen the risk of heart disease.

One area where there has been a success with omega-3s in pill form is using prescription strength fish oils to lower triglycerides. It may be that only people with high triglycerides benefit from fish oil and they need it in high doses, but that isn't clear at this time. However, a can of sardines, mackerel or anchovies every day can lower triglycerides just as well as the prescription fish oil capsules.

By lowering inflammation, fish oils may also reduce the risk of certain cancers as well.

It may be the case that consuming the whole fish is important for fighting heart disease, rather than getting the oils in pill form that may leave out some unknown cofactors.

Fatty fish also helps you feel satiated with a meal in a way that lean meat will not. Although salmon isn't consumed in the Mediterranean region, it's a perfectly acceptable food since it has a similar nutrition profile to sardines and mackerel.

## Health benefits of nuts and seeds

Nuts and seeds provide many key nutrients that lead to a healthier lifestyle. At the forefront of the many health benefits of nuts is that like olive oil, nuts contain a large amount of healthy monounsaturated fat. Nuts also contain a large number of minerals, in particular, they are good sources of potassium, magnesium, and some nuts have significant amounts of calcium. If you recall from our discussion about the origins of the DASH diet, nuts have many of the nutrients that are necessary to bring your electrolytes into balance and achieve or maintain healthy blood pressure levels. The monounsaturated fats found in nuts also contribute to health in the same way that olive oil contributes to health, helping to reduce inflammation and improve blood lipids. Nuts are high in calories, so they are restricted on the DASH diet. On a Mediterranean diet, you can eat as many as you like provided that you don't overeat (eat past being full).

The monounsaturated fats found in nuts help lower bad cholesterol. In fact, studies that examine the consumption of nuts have found that people who eat nuts on a daily basis have lower rates of heart attacks and stroke.

In addition to supplying vital minerals, nuts are also a good source of vitamin E. Nuts also supply large amounts of dietary fiber, making them a good adjunct to whole grains, fruits, and vegetables.

Some nuts, in particular walnuts, contain a form of omega-3 fatty acids. However, the form of omega-3 fats in plants and in this case nuts is not utilized by the body as easily as the omega-3 fats found in fish. When seeking omega-3 fat you should eat fish, but nuts should be consumed for other reasons.

Nuts also contain an amino acid called L-arginine. This little fellow plays an important role in keeping your arteries healthy, they make your arteries more flexible and lowers the occurrence of blot clots.

Good nuts to consume include almonds, walnuts, pecans, pistachios, and macadamia nuts. Cashews have a bit of carb in them so you might try consuming them less often. In any case, snacking on a handful of nuts daily is a good way to maintain lifelong health. You can also use nuts and seeds to top off salads or include them with stir-fried vegetables.

## The Benefits of Red Wine

Red wine contains many phytonutrients and anti-oxidants. Moderate consumption of alcohol has even been shown to increase lifespan. This effect is known as the "J-curve". That is, relative to moderate drinkers, those who don't drink at all have an elevated risk of death. While there is a sweet spot where you get the most benefit, drinking beyond that begins to increase your risk of cancer and other problems like stomach ulcers and bleeding. So people who are heavy drinkers tend to have a much higher risk of death as compared to people who don't drink or moderate drinkers.

Red wine has also been associated with a lower risk of a heart attack. France has low death rates due to heart disease despite high fat consumption, and red wine is believed to be the reason. It might raise HDL cholesterol slightly, and also thins the blood a little bit that may reduce the risk of blood clots that could cause heart attacks and strokes (when consumed in moderation, heavy drinkers have a serious risk of internal bleeding).

Some studies have also shown that red wine can help maintain healthy levels of omega-3 fats and maintain healthy blood sugar levels.

However, it almost goes without saying – if you don't drink now you're probably better off not starting. And if you have problems controlling alcohol consumption you probably shouldn't drink at all.

## *Foods You Can Eat on the Mediterranean Diet*

Let's go through a comprehensive list of foods you can eat on the Mediterranean diet. Unlike the DASH diet, no portion sizes are given, and generally, there aren't really daily recommended portions, just general guidelines. After all, it's based on a natural way of eating and not on a diet that was concocted by doctors in a research lab.

- Eat as many fruit and vegetables as you like, daily. This not only includes leafy green vegetables and broccoli but also sweet potatoes and even regular potatoes.
- Berries are allowed on the Mediterranean diet, including blueberries, strawberries, blackberries, and raspberries.
- Eat as many whole grains as you like, daily. This can include whole grain bread, pasta, quinoa, brown rice, wild rice, oats, and bran.
- You can use beans and legumes as a protein source in any meal. Garbanzo beans (sometimes called chickpeas) are very popular throughout the Mediterranean region.
- Consume fatty fish at least twice per week, but you can consume it daily or even multiple times a day.

- Low-fat seafood like cod, lobster, clams, scallops, and shrimp can be consumed with any meal.
- Nuts and seeds can be eaten daily.
- You can consume moderate portions of poultry, eggs, and dairy like yogurt and cheese about once a week or maybe twice a week. Poultry can be of any variety, including chicken, turkey, and duck.
- Red meat –specifically beef, lamb, and pork is permitted, but consumed on an occasional basis (once a week or less).
- Sweets are allowed on an occasional basis.
- Red wine can be consumed daily, in moderate amounts. That means 1 daily glass for women and 1-2 for men.
- Drink water liberally.
- Coffee and tea are permitted.

While there aren't specific portion rules, many people who follow a Mediterranean diet use a plate portioned out for guidance. The general rules are:

- Fill half the plate with vegetables.
- Fill a quarter of the plate with legumes, beans, and fruits.

- Fill a quarter of the plate with meat

## Foods Avoided on the Mediterranean Diet

Like the DASH diet, the Mediterranean diet isn't really a diet of exclusion, so there isn't really a long list of things to avoid and it's not a diet like keto where entire food groups are banned for life. Rather certain foods are consumed in moderation, on an occasional basis.

## The Science behind the Mediterranean diet

The Mediterranean diet promotes health in several ways. These are:

- It encourages weight loss. Maintaining healthy weight levels reduces the risk of heart disease, diabetes, stroke, and many cancers.
- The Mediterranean diet, primarily through fish oil, nuts, and olive oil, helps keep inflammation at bay. The science shows that inflammation is a major problem for a wide variety of health conditions and diseases, from arthritis to cancer to heart disease.
- The Mediterranean diet will reduce triglycerides, cutting the risk of heart disease significantly.

- The Mediterranean may reduce LDL or bad cholesterol. It does this directly through the consumption of olive oil, fiber, nuts, and fish, and also indirectly by reducing the intake of saturated fats found in animal meats.
- The Mediterranean diet may help keep your arteries young and supple, which means they will respond more easily to stress and stay young. This reduces the risk of heart attack and stroke.
- The Mediterranean diet reduces the risk of developing type 2 diabetes.

Researchers have compared the Mediterranean diet in studies to vegan, low fat, and low carb diets. Recent studies have shown that in comparison with vegan and low-fat diets, the Mediterranean diet was more effective at reducing A1C, which is a long term marker for high blood sugar.

# Chapter 4: Combining the DASH and Mediterranean Diets

Now we know what the DASH and Mediterranean diets are. We've seen that they have many similarities and some differences. You might be shaking your head, wondering if the differences are too great to overcome. For example, on the Mediterranean diet, you can chow down nuts until you're full, but the DASH diet is very strict, having you eat almost like you're a little white rabbit taking a couple of nibbles and calling it a day.

However, the similarities between the diets suggest that a new, better diet can be created by merging the two together. Let's start from first principles. Both diets reject the consumption of fast foods, junk food, packaged food, and processed foods. Both diets promote the consumption of whole, natural foods.

When it comes to health effects, there is some overlap as well. It's fair to say that the DASH diet is better at lowering blood pressure. However, the Mediterranean diet is probably better at reducing the risk of heart related diseases and stroke. In fact, we know that to be true, since the DASH diet is a low-fat diet, and in direct comparison with low-fat diets, superior outcomes have been demonstrating for the Mediterranean diet.

Both are good for weight loss. So how do we do it? How do we combine these two successful diets into one diet that can produce better health outcomes? Let's dive in.

### *Applying The DASH Basics with a Mediterranean Flair and Modifying the DASH/ Mediterranean diets*

Our approach is going to be simple. Let's go over the DASH basics.

- Limit sodium intake. The DASH diet is not a no-salt diet but limits salt to 2,300 mg per day for the standard DASH diet, and 1,500 mg per day for the low-sodium version of the DASH diet.
- Fruits and vegetables are the items consumed in the greatest quantity.
- Whole grains are consumed liberally, but not as much as fruits and vegetables.
- Lean meats are consumed in moderation.

- Dairy – normally low fat is consumed 2-3 times per day.
- Nuts, seeds, beans, and legumes are consumed once per day.
- Oils, dressings, and condiments are consumed in moderation.
- Sweets are consumed occasionally.
- For all categories, portion sizes are given in specific amounts along with numbers of portions per day.
- Red wine and other alcoholic drinks aren't necessarily banned, but they are mildly discouraged because they might raise blood pressure.

So how are we going to combine these rules with the Mediterranean diet? In fact, we get a long way toward the goal by simply moderating salt intake on the Mediterranean diet.

One difference between the Mediterranean diet and the DASH diet is the level of dairy consumption. The DASH diet allows more consumption of dairy; on the Mediterranean diet dairy products are consumed occasionally, while the DASH diet encourages daily consumption of dairy products in modest quantities.

Why you may ask, is that so?

The reason is the fundamental goal behind the DASH diet. You will recall that the DASH diet was designed to bring minerals that impact blood pressure into balance. Have you read the nutrition facts label on a carton of milk lately? Well if you did you'd know that one cup of milk contains:

- 366 mg of potassium
- 107 mg of sodium
- 30% of daily required calcium
- 6% of daily required magnesium

Now, if you're lactose intolerant, then downing a glass of milk each day isn't in the cards. But for those that aren't lactose intolerant, milk is a mineral powerhouse! Remember the goal is to bring sodium, potassium, calcium, and magnesium into balance for optimal blood pressure function. Milk has them all – in a single glass. It's like a natural drug the blood pressure doctor ordered!

Notice that in a glass of milk – there is some sodium. But there is more potassium. You need to get sodium, but you need more potassium than sodium. We've been harping on the amount of sodium you should have per day – in particular, that the average American consumes about 3,500 mg per day, but the doctors that came up with the DASH diet say we should be eating about 2,300 mg per day, but how much potassium? We haven't said yet, and it's time to address this problem.

It's recommended that you consume between 3,500-4,700 mg of potassium per day. So you're supposed to be getting more potassium each day than you're getting sodium. A cup of milk provides 3.4 times as much potassium as it does sodium. Unless you're going to salt your milk, drinking some milk is a good addition to your diet to help control your blood pressure.

Now for fun let's compare that to the ratio of the highest recommended level of potassium to the low-sodium recommendations of the DASH diet, which is 1,500 mg per day.

$$4,700/1,500 = 3.1$$

So it's about in the same ballpark as milk sounds like milk is a go.

We should also note that milk provides calcium, which is also important for proper management of blood pressure, and that you can get these nutrients from yogurt as well.

Now we've also been harping on the fact that the Mediterranean diet is a high-fat diet, at least relatively speaking, while the DASH diet is a low-fat diet. However, some interesting studies were done that allowed DASH dieters to consume full-fat varieties of dairy products. Guess what they found? To everyone's surprise, they found that the full-fat dairy DASH dieters had better blood lipid results than people following the standard DASH diet.

So here is the rub. We can modify the Mediterranean diet by allowing daily consumption of some dairy products in moderation. Second, since we're advocating the higher fat Mediterranean diet, we can incorporate full-fat dairy products as long as they're consumed in moderation. If you look at a cup of milk, whole milk contains 4.6 g of saturated fat. However, it also contains 2 g of monounsaturated fat (think back to – olive oil and nuts) and 0.5 g of polyunsaturated fat. So milk is not all bad, but it does load up on saturated fat so we'll consume it in moderation. If you can afford it and it's available in your area, purchase milk from pasture-raised, grass-fed cows.

So far we've taken two steps to modify the Mediterranean diet to make it more DASH-like:

- Keep track of sodium intake, and limit to 2,300 mg or so per day.
- Increase dairy consumption to 2-3 small servings per day, as opposed to it being a once in a while thing.

Because of the increased calories, you might see by consuming dairy daily, they should be cut somewhere else. So as part of the merger of the two diets, we'll limit the consumption of fruits and vegetables, using the rule given in the DASH diet, but since sugar calories come from fruit, weighted toward vegetables. We'll reduce the number of fruit servings allowed per day on the DASH diet from 4-5 to 3 servings per day. Also while you should watch your consumption of starchy vegetables like sweet potatoes, you can eat leafy greens, broccoli, celery, and asparagus with near reckless abandon. If you limit most of your vegetable consumption to greens, then incorporating more calories with dairy shouldn't be a problem.

Given the massive benefits to health that have been demonstrated for olive oil, nuts, seeds, and fish oil, it seems like a bad move to try and limit their consumption when trying to combine the DASH and Mediterranean diets. In fact, that would nearly completely destroy the spirit of the Mediterranean diet whose identity is practically synonymous with olive oil. That means the DASH diet strict limits on oil, salad dressings and the like will be discarded. It doesn't make sense after learning that we should practically drink olive oil that we should be limiting oil to a tbsp. a day as its recommended by the DASH diet. However since adding extra oil also means added calories, we should cut back a little somewhere else.

Whole grains and carbs are a big source of calories, so it makes sense to adopt the DASH diet limits here. So we'll limit grains to 7-8 servings per day. We'll also follow the serving guidelines of the DASH diet, and take one serving of whole grains to be 1 slice of bread, a ½ cup of pasta, a ½ cup of rice or other grains, and a ½ cup of cereal.

When it comes to proteins, beans, and legumes, we will also relax some rules of the DASH diet. Remember that the

DASH diet allows 0-2 servings of meat per day, and 1 serving of nuts or beans/legumes or seeds per day. We're going to require 1 serving of nuts or seeds per day and allow up to 3 servings per day of meat, fish/seafood, and up to 3 servings per day of beans and legumes (recall the Mediterranean diet plate, which allows ¼ of the plate to be filled with fruits, beans, and legumes – that plate applies to every meal.

Another principle from the DASH diet we'll adopt is strict control of sweets. Rules for consumption of sweets on the Mediterranean diet are vague, so to put some teeth into them we'll limit consumption of sweets to 5 servings per week, but allow full-fat varieties of yogurt with fruit, frozen yogurt, and yes, ice cream, with ½ cup sizes per serving.

Finally, let's bring the lovely avocado to mind. Have you looked at the nutrition fact sheet for avocados lately? Probably not so let's list a few facts about avocadoes here:

- One medium avocado contains 20 grams of monounsaturated fat.
- An avocado contains 975 mg of potassium and only 14 mg of sodium.

- One avocado has 17 grams of carbohydrates, but 13 of them (that would be 77%) are fiber.
- One avocado supplies 33% of your daily vitamin C needs.
- One avocado supplies 14% of your daily magnesium requirements.

It should be clear by now that avocados are a nutritional powerhouse. And even though they satisfy many of the stated requirements of the DASH diet – that is bringing your minerals that influence blood pressure into balance by increasing potassium and magnesium, they are expected to be consumed in small amounts on DASH. Why? Because of the high-fat content.

That's a bad way to look at things – and if the first rule of merging DASH with the Mediterranean diet is to pump up the fat – if you can do that *and* get a massive dose of potassium and magnesium – it seems like including avocados is a far better idea than limiting their consumption. We could even make it a rule that you'll have to consume avocados, but of course, that won't work for everyone.

So let's take a step back and summarize. We're completely rejecting the low-fat principles of the DASH diet. Fat not only provides health benefits as described for olive oil and fish oil, but it also helps you get satiated so that you don't overeat.

However, we're going to apply some DASH rules. Namely, we're going to place limits on consumption of fruits and vegetables, whole grains, dairy, and sweets as specified by the DASH diet, and use the 2,300 mg limit of sodium. If you have issues with blood pressure you may want to try the 1,500 mg sodium limit, but discuss with your doctor first.

### *Rules of the DASH-Mediterranean Solution*

- Eat three meals per day, with 1-3 snacks. You can snack on nuts, seeds, or small amounts of cheese.
- Eat 8-10 servings of fruits and vegetables daily. Limit servings of fruit to 3 per day. A serving of fruit is one medium-sized fruit (think orange or apple), a ½ cup of frozen, fresh, or dried fruits, and a ¼ cup of fruit juice.
- If you like avocados, make one of your servings of fruit (yes, avocado is a fruit) avocado.

- Eat 6-8 servings per day of whole grains. A serving of whole grains is 1 slice of bread, a ½ cup of pasta, a ½ cup of rice, or a ½ cup of cereal.
- Eat meat up to 3 times per day, but you can substitute beans and legumes for meat in some of your meals. Excellent sources of protein include garbanzo beans and kidney beans.
- Eat a minimum of 2 servings of fish per week. If you're OK with eating fish, eat 3-5 times per week or even daily servings of fish.
-  Be sure to eat breakfast, and include a bit of protein with breakfast.
- Eat one serving of nuts or seeds per day.
- Have 2-3 moderate servings of full-fat dairy per day. One cup of milk or yogurt, or some small amounts of cheese.
- Eat eggs, up to 4 times per week, can add egg whites 2 times per week beyond the 4 egg limit.
- No limits on condiments, mayo, oils, and dressings, provided that they are either olive oil or avocado oil. Mayo based on olive oil and avocado oil is available at most grocery stores.
- Eat five servings of sweets per week, maximum in ½ cup servings. Full-fat varieties allowed.

- Drink red wine in moderation.
- You should also exercise moderately 30 minutes per day.

## *Supercharged Benefits of the DASH-Mediterranean diet*

Earlier we discussed the health benefits of the DASH diet. Then we discussed the health benefits of the Mediterranean diet. Now let's look at the supercharged health benefits of combining these two diets.

### Fosters a healthy heart and maintains blood pressure levels

By incorporating heart-healthy monounsaturated fats and fish oils into the DASH diet framework, we can greatly improve overall heart health. Remember that the DASH diet helps maintain and control high blood pressure, which is the reason why arteries are damage and initiates the onslaught of heart disease. From what we know now, low-fat diets are only moderately protective against heart disease when compared with diets that replace carbohydrates and bad fats with good, healthy, unsaturated fats. Specifically, this diet may:

- Reduce your triglycerides (fish oil, nuts, avocados, and olive oil).
- Raise your HDL or "good" cholesterol (red wine, olive oil, fish oil).
- Lower your LDL or "bad" cholesterol (nuts, olive oil, avocados).
- Keep blood pressure in check (sodium limits, dairy, avocados, other fruits, and veggies)

**Reduced Inflammation**

We've talked about inflammation a bit already. Recall that the inflammation marker C - reactive protein or CRP is associated with a higher risk of heart disease. Inflammation is also associated with many diseases including cancer, inflammatory bowel disease, arthritis, and even cancer. It's been shown that a diet high in healthy fats, like the Mediterranean diet, can help reduce and control inflammation. Moreover, the antioxidants and phytonutrients found in plants also assist in keeping inflammation at bay. On the DASH-Mediterranean solution diet, you'll be getting the massive dose of antioxidants you normally get from the DASH diet by consuming large numbers of fruits and vegetables, you'll also be getting the benefits of reduced inflammation from the Mediterranean diet. Olive oil, avocados, and fish oil all contribute to reduced inflammation. Fish oil has been shown to reduce levels of pro-inflammatory molecules in the body called cytokines. In addition to causing an inflammatory response, cytokines are also involved in disastrous disease processes including the flu, hantavirus infections, and pneumonia. But with the DASH-Mediterranean diet, you'll get copious amounts of olive oil, avocados, nuts, fish oil, along with the fruits and vegetables from the DASH diet that will all work together to reduce inflammation.

## Lower Risk of Cancer

It's possible that the DASH-Mediterranean diet can help lessen the chances of multiple cancers. Already, we've seen that the diet reduces inflammation throughout the body. Inflammation can also raise your risk of cancer, in addition to heart disease. By avoiding processed foods, the diet also encourages a healthier mode of eating that reduces your risk of cancer. Although we take a more liberal approach to eat meat on the combo diet as opposed to the DASH diet alone, mainly to increase fish consumption and increase consumption of healthy oils, on the DASH-Mediterranean solution diet you should avoid processed meats. Yes, they can be consumed once in a while, however, foods loaded with nitrates and nitrates may increase the risk of cancer. Examples include bacon, salami, and pepperoni, among others. You can't entirely prevent cancer as far as we know right now, but cancer experts repeatedly emphasize that you do the following:

- Eat a lot of fiber.
- Eat copious amounts of fruits and vegetables.
- Consume foods that reduce inflammation.

You will quickly note that the DASH-Mediterranean solution diet immediately addresses all three of these recommendations. You can get plenty of fiber from leafy greens, fruits, avocados, nuts, and seeds, as well as from whole grains. We're recommending 8-10 servings a day of fruits and vegetables, which is well above the five servings per day normally recommended by medical professionals. Olive oil, avocados, nuts, seeds, and fatty fish will work to reduce inflammation.

## Mental Focus and Brain Health

If you've spent any amount of time eating the standard American diet, then there is no doubt you've experienced brain fog. You've also probably experienced a blood sugar crash. Food that is based on simple carbohydrates gets "burned off" quickly, and without enough fuel, your brain begins to operate in a fog.

The DASH diet really doesn't address this. Although the carbohydrates consumed in the standard DASH diet are better – simple, unrefined carbs are replaced by healthier whole grains – the DASH diet severely restricts fat. Although at the time of the diet this was believed to be the best approach for health, we've since learned that consuming fat is good for you. Fat does a lot of things, but in the context of mental focus what fat does is it helps generate long term, sustainable energy.

Think about it – do you feel more satisfied eating a bowl of white rice, or a bowl of brown rice with salmon doused in olive oil. The latter will definitely sustain you longer throughout the day and help you focus. Eating avocados and nuts can also help give you sustained, and strong energy levels that help bring mental clarity and focus.

Moreover, the omega-3 fats found in fish have been shown to promote the integrity of the brain. It's even been reported that omega-3 fats can help improve mood and mental health, fighting depression and the kind of mood swings found with bipolar disorder.

## Reduced Insulin Resistance

Remember that earlier we discussed the problem of insulin resistance. Since insulin is tied to carbohydrate consumption, when you begin to weight your diet more toward healthy fats and proteins, your body needs less insulin. With the DASH diet, it's not clear that insulin resistance can be improved by the diet because not only is it heavily carbohydrate-based, it also encourages the consumption of 4-5 fruits per day. Fruits are fine and healthy, but they also contain simple sugars that your body will convert into blood glucose, requiring an insulin response.

With the DASH-Mediterranean diet, however, we're replacing some of the calories consumed with fruits and grains with fat from olive oil, avocados, nuts, and fish oil (by the way – consider olives as a serving of fruit during the day and get even more olive oil while consuming fruit). When you cut back on fruits and eat more healthy fats, you're going to require less of an insulin response. That implies the DASH-Mediterranean diet will help improve insulin resistance.

Reducing insulin resistance, and consuming a diet that includes calories weighted more towards oils and fats, will also give your pancreas a bit of a rest, helping overall health.

**Prevent and in some cases reverse type 2 diabetes**

By replacing carbohydrate consumption, especially consumption of refined carbohydrates with fats and healthy proteins, you can greatly improve the health of people who are suffering from pre-diabetes. By reversing insulin resistance and encouraging weight loss, and making your pancreas do less work if you're suffering from pre-diabetes you're going to see improvements in your fasting blood sugars. Moreover, you'll avoid the organ damaging blood sugar spikes that occur when following a standard American diet. Depending on how far your type 2 diabetes has progressed, those in the earlier stages may be able to repair their metabolism and massively improve their blood sugar and A1C values, possibly getting off medications. It's too hopeful to say that the diet offers a possibility of curing diabetes, but it does provide a potentially useful tool for managing it.

## Look and Feel Younger

It seems a stretch, but a diet high in olive oil can help improve skin tone and reduce wrinkles. In addition, you're likely to feel increased levels of energy on the diet.

# Chapter 5: Good Fats, Bad Fats, and the DASH-Mediterranean Solution

For years, we were told that fat should be avoided altogether, the lower the fat contents in your diet the better. This may have culminated with the diet developed by Dr. Dean Ornish, a cardiologist who advised eating less than 10% of your calories from fat.

The DASH diet was created during this era, so it too is a low-fat diet. However, as we've noted before since that time we've discovered that after all, fats aren't bad for you. The picture is more complicated than thought previously, some fats aren't black and white while others are. Let's look at the details.

## Good Fats vs. Bad Fats

In the past couple of decades, scientists began to realize that some fats are actually good for you. This began when people began to take reports that eating fish reduced heart attacks seriously. Some cultures that ate a lot of fish were consuming tons of fish fat, yet they had very low rates of heart disease.

Another indication that fats weren't necessarily bad was the observation, later backed by controlled research, that eating nuts, which are mostly fat, improved cardiovascular health, reduced inflammation, and reduced the risk of death from all causes. As we've seen, similar results were found for olive oil.

However, there are bad fats. For decades, public enemy number one has been saturated fats. The reason was the belief in the cholesterol hypothesis. When you eat saturated fat, the liver converts it into cholesterol. So the more meat you eat the higher your cholesterol. We now know that the picture is more complicated than originally thought, so we'll put saturated fat in the "neutral" category.

The most obvious bad fat is artificially produced trans-fats. These are not to be confused with trans-fats that occur naturally in beef. Artificially produced trans-fats are made in a laboratory and were used for decades in deep-frying and to add fat to processed foods. Trans-fats were preferred by the junk food community because they had a stable shelf-life. Artificially produced trans-fats hit your blood lipids across all fronts. They lower your good, or HDL cholesterol. They raise your bad, or LDL cholesterol. They may even raise triglycerides. Medical professionals have recommended not consuming more than one gram per day. In fact, the U.S. government finally banned the use of trans-fats, although food companies that use them were given a grace period of several years to replace them.

Another set of bad fats includes vegetable oils. This category absolutely does not include olive oil and avocado oil. However, corn, safflower, soybean, and canola oil are bad fats. These oils are mainly omega-6 fats. While you do need some omega-6 fats in your diet, they are pro-inflammatory and you certainly don't want to be adding extra by cooking in corn oil. Unfortunately in their zeal to get away from animal fat in the 1960s and 1970s, health experts actually convinced the public to use copious amounts of these unhealthy oils. Who knows how much health damage was caused by this decision.

To summarize, the bad fats include:
- Artificially produced trans-fats.
- Omega-6 heavy vegetable oils. A partial list is canola, corn, sunflower, safflower, and soybean oil.

Saturated fat – which is found in animal products (including fish by the way) and in lower amounts in vegetable products (especially coconut and palm oil) is a neutral fat. To determine if it's harmful you need to examine the rest of the diet and check triglycerides (low triglycerides, don't worry about it).

Good fats include:

- Olive oil
- Avocados and avocado oil
- Fish oil
- Fats found in nuts

## Avoiding Trans Fats and Processed Foods

The best way to avoid trans-fats is to check labels on processed foods. The US Government has required that food manufacturers phase them out.

## Healthy Fats of the Mediterranean Diet

We've seen that the Mediterranean diet is full of healthy fats including olive oil, avocados, and monounsaturated fats found in nuts and seeds, and fish oils.

## How the Mediterranean Diet Forces a Rethink on Fats

The Mediterranean diet helped force researchers into a re-evaluation of the role of fats in the diet. Had the Mediterranean diet not existed, we might never have come this far. The health of people who were following the diet as a matter of tradition, and having superior health outcomes despite consuming copious amounts of fats and oils, forced researchers to take a closer look. When they did, they discovered that monounsaturated fats and fish oils decrease inflammation and even improve blood markers that are associated with heart disease.

# Chapter 6: Carbs, Dairy, and Proteins

Now let's have a look at the other important macros in the diet, carbs, and proteins. We'll also take a look at the dairy.

## *What is the Glycemic Index*

In recent years, carbs have become the new devil, replacing fat in that dietary role. Many low carb fads have hit the market, starting with the Atkins diet, which emphasized limiting carbs to 20 grams per day. This was followed in the 1990s by the South Beach Diet, which was a modernized knock-off of the Atkins diet and essentially a marketing ploy. Then, a new fad was started when an anthropologist specializing in pre-history attempted to devise a diet based on how ice age hunter-gatherer tribes ate, the theory that this is what our bodies were designed to eat. While also low carb, it wasn't as radical as the Atkins diet. It soon became known as the paleo diet and also goes by the name primal. Lately, the keto or ketogenic diet, which is like Atkins but based on consuming specific amounts of fat, has taken the stage. Some people are also following the carnivore diet, which even eliminates the small amounts of carbohydrates consumed on Atkins and Keto diets.

Those diets may work for some people, but they aren't for everyone. If you're reading this book you're probably more interested in following a diet that is based on moderation, rather than eliminating entire food groups.

With that in mind, if you're going to eat carbohydrates then you want to understand them and how the human body reacts to digesting them. One measure of the body's response is the glycemic index of a carbohydrate-based food item. In short, the glycemic index measures how the body responds to the carbohydrate. A high glycemic index means that blood sugar will rise substantially after eating the food, while a low glycemic index means that blood sugar won't go up very much. If you're pre-diabetic or have type 2 diabetes, knowing the glycemic indices of food is very useful information.

The scale for the glycemic index is 0-100. Eating pure olive oil would be about 3, it won't have any effect on your blood sugar. On the other hand, consuming pure glucose will cause it to shoot up, so glucose is selected to set the baseline with a score of 100. You can go online and search for the glycemic index to get a comprehensive listing.

Here are some values for specific foods:

- Avocado: 6
- Peanuts: 14
- Apple: 38
- Brown rice: 55
- Honey: 55
- White rice: 64
- Raisins: 64
- Table sugar: 68
- Watermelon: 72
- Baked potato: 85

As you can see from this partial list, eating some foods is worse than others, and surprisingly some foods you might think of as more healthy real foods, like watermelon and baked potatoes, are worse than just downing pure table sugar. Would you believe that white rice had the same impact as honey?

## *Eating Whole Grains*

The brown rice versus white rice comparison – with white rice being equivalent to honey – shows that eating whole grains is better. A slice of white bread has a glycemic index of 73, while a slice of whole grain bread has a glycemic index of about 51. This clearly demonstrates that whole grain foods will have less of an impact on your blood sugar than refined carbohydrates.

However, you should consider doing your own tests. Get a blood sugar monitor and find out what your blood sugar does in response to eating certain foods. To do this test your blood sugar immediately before eating, and then test it again two hours after eating. To zero in on specific foods you should only eat one food item for the test (so for example a slice of bread).

If you find your blood sugar levels go up quite a bit even when eating whole grains and whole fruits, you can improve your diet by reducing your consumption of these foods and replacing them with something else. A person with problems controlling their blood sugar even with whole wheat pasta might substitute an avocado or garbanzo beans in their place, for example.

### *Dairy on the DASH-Mediterranean Solution*

Let's take a look at the glycemic index for a few dairy items:

- Whole milk: 27
- Skim milk: 32
- Yogurt with fruit: 40
- Vanilla ice cream: 38
- Natural yogurt: 28

Cheese tends to have a very low GI, so we'll ignore it here. You see that whole milk is a bit better than skim milk, and yogurt with fruit is the highest, which is why the DASH diet limits consumption of yogurt containing fruit. You may find it surprising that vanilla ice cream actually scores better than yogurt containing fruit.

## Acceptable Protein Sources

Acceptable protein sources on the DASH-Mediterranean diet solution are basically the same as you'd expect from either diet. The list of acceptable protein sources includes:

- Beans and legumes
- Fish and seafood of any kind
- Poultry, in moderation, preferably with skin removed
- Beef in moderation
- Pork in moderation

- Lamb occasionally

Avoid processed meats.

## Getting the Right Amounts of Carbs and Proteins

A serving of protein with each meal is generally considered around 4 ounces on the DASH diet, but we will follow the plate rule used on the Mediterranean diet. Fill about a quarter of your plate with protein, half with vegetables. That leaves a quarter of your plate to fill with either whole grains, fruits, or beans/legumes or some combination of them.

# Chapter 7: Phase One- Reset Your Metabolism in Two Weeks

Now, it's time to get into the nitty-gritty of actually implementing the diet. For the first two weeks, we'll keep things fairly simple and restrict portions. The purpose of this is two-fold. First off, we don't want to be overwhelmed with details when starting the new diet, so we'll offer very simple meal suggestions for the first seven days to help you get started. Second, we'll limit portions a little bit for the first 7-14 days, so that you can get going with weight loss. However the meals we suggest should be pretty satisfying for most people, so they won't leave you feeling hungry.

Let's put together some basic shopping lists, beginning with meat. We'll suggest 3 servings of fish per week for the first 14 days. In phase one, we won't go as heavy on the dairy.

**Meat shopping list**
- Salmon
- Trout
- Canned sardines
- Skinless + Boneless chicken breasts

- Skinless + Boneless chicken thighs
- 85% lean ground beef or ground turkey
- Pork loin
- Eggs
- Smoked salmon

## Beans and Legumes

- 3 cans of garbanzo beans
- 1 can kidney beans
- Lentils
- Peanuts

## Nuts and seeds

- Pre-packed Planters heart-healthy nut mix, eat one bag per day.
- Unsalted walnuts
- Unsalted pumpkin seeds
- Unsalted almond or walnut butter

## Dairy

- Grass-Fed Whole milk
- Swiss cheese
- Parmesan cheese

- Unsweetened yogurt

## Fruits and vegetables

- Spinach (no limits to greens)
- Arugula
- Tomatoes
- Onions
- Garlic
- Strawberries
- Blackberries
- Blueberries
- Raspberries
- Bananas (great source of potassium)
- Avocados
- Spring mix
- Apples
- Cucumbers
- Bell peppers
- Asparagus
- Celery
- Kale

## Whole grains

- Whole wheat pasta
- Whole grain bread
- Wild rice
- Brown rice
- Steel cut oats
- Quinoa

## Oils and dressings

- Extra-Virgin Olive oil
- Avocado oil
- Olive or Avocado based mayo
- Low sodium mustard
- Vinegar
- Olive oil and vinegar salad dressing
- Balsamic vinegar salad dressing
- Any low or no-sodium spices (cumin, basil, cayenne pepper, lemon pepper, garlic powder, thyme, etc.)

## A 14 Day Reset

Jumping into this diet will be a shock to your body but you probably won't notice it, other than feeling better. The fact is this style of diet is far more natural and actually closer to what you're used to than something like the keto diet, which is a very major shift. However, making a major change always causes challenges. A traditional Mediterranean diet is easier to adjust to because on the DASH diet you're going to be doing a lot of salt restriction. The main challenge to the DASH-Mediterranean diet will be in preparing your meals and finding tasty substitutes you can use to season your food and make it tasty without using salt. Living in the American culture, salt has been the go-to seasoning device for decades, and this can be a hard habit to break. However, don't forget that you can use some salt, but you should be keeping track of the amounts consumed. In the original study, participants were given salt packets that contained 200 mg of salt to season their food with. You can jump online to see if you can get pre-measured salt packets to allow you to season some of your food with salt and you'll have an exact idea of how much you're adding. However remember that all food has some sodium in it – so you need to keep track of that too. Don't just load up on a bunch of 200 mg salt packets and use them up until you reach 2,300 mg or even 1,500 mg – be sure to count the sodium in a chicken breast and so on.

Here are some sodium levels in food to help you track your total daily intake:

- Skinless chicken breast 1 lb.: 38 mg
- Skinless chicken thigh: 101 mg
- Atlantic salmon, 3 oz portion: 50 mg
- Whole wheat bread, 1 slice: 112 mg
- Barilla whole grain pasta: 0 mg
- Avocado: 6 mg
- 1 cup of whole milk: 105 mg

Be sure to drink enough water when starting your new diet. Often people are not getting enough water to begin with, and when making a major change in food consumption this will magnify the negative effects that may have been previously under the radar. It's a cliché by now, but drink 8 glasses of water a day. Some people may need even more. If you're a coffee and tea drinker (and a wine drinker at night) remember that these beverages are natural diuretics and you're going to need to drink some water to replace what's lost.

### Blood Sugar and Phase One

If you're pre-diabetic or diabetic, be sure to follow your blood sugar closely when making major dietary changes. Keep track of your numbers so that you know how your body responds to new foods in your diet. You may also find that the foods you've eaten in the past might affect you differently when presented to your body in new combinations.

Also, be sure to keep track of your blood pressure – especially if you've already been diagnosed with hypertension and are on medication. Reducing your salt intake significantly might have a large impact on your blood pressure – so be aware of feeling dizzy or other symptoms that might actually indicate your readings might be getting too low.

### Proportions and Foods for Phase One

Remember the following rules:

- Fill half your plate with vegetables (your choice).
- Don't eat too many starchy vegetables like sweet potatoes.
- Fill one-quarter of your plate with meat.

- Fill one-quarter of your plate with whole grains, fruits, beans, and legumes.
- Eat dairy 2-3 times per day. It can be 1 cup of milk and a serving of yogurt or cheese, or 2 cups of milk, your choice.
- Follow the rules for portions consumed per day we outlined earlier.

Another tip is to eat the colors of the rainbow each day. Fruits and vegetables run through all the colors – from deep purple blackberries to yellow bananas and red bell peppers. The colors aren't accidental, they indicate what chemicals and anti-oxidants are contained in the fruit or vegetable. The more colors you're getting every day, the healthier your diet is. Since we're aiming for a high level of consumption of fruits and vegetables on this diet, you shouldn't have too much problem filling your plate with lots of colors.

Another good rule is to eat protein with your breakfast. These days not enough breakfast is a plague that infects people as much as drinking too little water. You don't have to cook a huge complicated meal for breakfast, it could be as simple as eating an egg with your cereal. Another suggestion that makes a great fulfilling breakfast is a serving of smoked salmon, and that will also help you load up on omega-3 fats to start your day.

Getting enough exercise will help you get the most out of the DASH-Mediterranean diet. Moderate exercise is enough for most people, so if you're not the kind of person that wants to hit the gym and peddle as fast as possible for an hour until you're drenched in sweat, don't be put off by the idea. A simple 30-minute walk at a moderate pace can go a long way toward improving your health if you've been living a sedentary lifestyle. For those who are more ambitious, adding some strength training can help and you can look into taking up jogging, running on a treadmill or an outdoor activity like mountain biking. Swimming is also an excellent exercise choice. It really doesn't matter what specific exercise routine you select – the point is to get moving a few days a week. Pick an exercise activity that you enjoy. If you find something that you find to be fun you're more likely to stick with it.

Exercise suggestions:

- 30-minute walk, five days per week
- Swimming

- Cycling
- Jogging
- Mountain biking
- Walk the dog daily
- Hiking on mountain or nature trails
- Elliptical
- Rowing machine
- Pilates
- Yoga

Getting enough sleep is another one of those things that people don't get enough of, like drinking water. To maintain good health it's a good idea to keep your sleep rhythms relatively constant and to get a good 6-8 hours of sleep per night. Everyone is different, so for some folks getting only 6 hours of sleep can be more than sufficient, while others will be dragging. Make sure that you get the amount of sleep that works best for you.

Stress reduction is important as well. When you're under chronic stress, whether it's worrying about problems at work, being unable to pay bills or marital problems, your health suffers. It turns out that being constantly stressed can increase levels of inflammation throughout the body. If you're looking into adopting the DASH-Mediterranean diet, then you're looking to improve your health. While what you put in your mouth is certainly very important, don't neglect what's going on in your mental life either. The body works in a feedback loop with the brain, and when you're feeling a lot of stress the body reacts.

Sometimes stress is over events or situations we don't have immediate control over if we can control it at all. Maybe you have a large credit card debt that is hard to pay off right now. Rather than sitting around stressed out about it constantly – which accomplishes nothing – you should focus on your health instead. One good suggestion is to take up yoga twice a week. Although we listed yoga as an exercise activity – and it is – yoga is also great for promoting relaxation and reducing stress. You can also add a daily meditation or prayer session to your day. If possible, do that first thing in the morning. People with young children at home or who face a long commute may find that difficult, but you can find some small time frame of 5-10 minutes a day where you can meditate and relax to help relieve stress. Deep breathing exercises throughout the day can help as well.

With many diets, starting a new diet can create stress with friends and family, in particular, if you are living with one or more people in your home who don't share your desire to embark on a new diet. The good thing about the DASH and Mediterranean diets is that they aren't really all that radical, so it shouldn't be too hard to get family members to go along. Eating out isn't too problematic either since many of the top options listed in this diet are available in most restaurants. One thing you can do is request no salt versions of a dish, and certainly avoid using the salt shaker. You can also request that the cook not use MSG on your meal, and substitute vegetables for unacceptable side items. Salmon is a popular item in just about any restaurant these days – but beware of high salt sauces, in particular, teriyaki sauce. In fact, the only restaurants that might cause you trouble are Chinese and Japanese restaurants. If possible, ask for low-sodium soy sauce.

It's also important to keep a good attitude and forgive yourself when you make transgressions on the diet – which are inevitable on occasion. Using the example we just talked about, you might get a craving for Chinese food or coworkers might drag you along for sushi. It's not going to be the end of the world if you eat one meal with high salt content. Rather than beating yourself up over it, go along and enjoy it and make up for it later. That is the beauty of this diet it's very adaptable.

Let's just say that for example, you end up eating sushi which will mean eating a lot of salt. Obviously, you can be very strict on the following day to make up for it, but you can also make up for it at your next meal.

- At your next meal, eat very low salt, as low as possible.
- Include items that will help keep everything in balance. Add a full avocado, for example.
- Eat some fruit which has zero or low sodium but lots of potassium, like an apple or an orange.
- Drink some extra water to help flush your system.

There is no need to be neurotic about it, as you can see from these suggestions moving on from mistakes is relatively easy. Another transgression people often face is having to eat sweets. Maybe you're at a birthday party. Do you want to be the annoying curmudgeon who is always talking about their special diet? Probably not –so you'll probably just take the piece of cake they offer you. Again, don't sweat it. If you get into a situation where you consume a lot of sweets:

- Count the cake as your five servings of sweets for the week, and don't eat anymore.
- At your next meal, reduce your carbs a bit and up your fat and protein intake instead. Substitute avocado or extra fish for some whole grains to temporarily reduce your carbs.
- Go fruitless for a day, and just get by eating seven or eight servings of vegetables. Opt for low carb vegetables like stir-fried spinach.
- Plan ahead. You'll digest sweets like cake and ice cream better by getting a good dose of fat beforehand. So if you have the choice, eat higher fat and low carb dish for your main meal prior to eating something like cake.

Finally, don't skip meals. The premise behind the Mediterranean diet is to be satisfied. That is one reason why fat is so important on the diet. Fat helps you feel satiated. When you're satiated, you eat less overall. That's why calorie counting isn't used on a Mediterranean diet. While the

DASH diet is more portion based, it also avoids counting calories.

Skipping meals can lead to problems. One issue some people have is a blood sugar crash when they haven't eaten in a long time. When that happens, they gorge themselves when they finally get to eat. You don't want to get into a situation where your body basically enters "starvation mode". Overeating is the inevitable result. By sticking to regular, satisfying, and well-portioned meals, you can ensure that you're not consuming too many calories without actually having to keep a diary where you're counting them up. The added fact that we've incorporated into the diet by adding the Mediterranean component will help keep you energized throughout the day. Do you have an urge to nap late in the afternoon? That might be because your diet is too dependent on carbohydrates. By eating a little less carbohydrate and substituting healthy fats, you'll find that you have more energy and that the energy is more sustainable. You want to keep your blood sugar from going up and down – and remember that fluctuating blood sugars also make people moody.

A quick word about spices. Since your taste buds are so used to heavy doses of salt, it might be tough to adjust to the new world of low-sodium eating. Some suggestions are to use a lot more citrus juice, in particular, lemon and lime juice. Lemon juice isn't just for fish, you can use it on the chicken to really flavor it nicely, for example. Lime juice serves the same purpose.

Another idea is to spice it up. Consider loading up on curry and cayenne pepper, unless it's absolutely against your taste buds. You might find, however, that after weaning off salt that these powerful spices start to become more appealing. Rubbing chicken with cayenne pepper or using curry in stir frying can really jump start your cooking. A wide variety of vegetables helps as well – and frying can unlock a wide range of flavors. Red and yellow onions and mushrooms are great for this purpose, as are basil and chives.

Think about "seasoning" your meats with vinegar instead of relying on salt. Balsamic vinegar is an excellent choice for this purpose. Use flavorful cheeses in moderation. Some people think that having read the recommendations of the DASH diet, that eating a one and a half ounce portion of cheese means cutting off a piece of cheddar and just eating it. If that's your though then broaden your thinking. You can have your serving of cheese as some grated parmesan on a baked chicken breast, for example. A tbsp. of parmesan has 76 mg of sodium, so adding some parmesan to your chicken will actually give it some salt flavor, without you adding extra salt to it. Chances are you're made parmesan chicken breast in the past, and you salted the chicken as well.

Finally, look for social support. Is there a friend at the office that you can have to join you on the diet? There is strength in numbers. You might both find that having a support buddy helps you stick to the diet – of course, the reality is with the foods that are on this kind of diet sticking to it isn't going to be very difficult for a lot of people, but if you need some social support to reach out and find it.

## *Suggested 7-Day Meal Plan for Phase One*

Our suggestion for the first seven days is to keep it simple. Getting bogged down in complicated recipes may make it hard to adjust to your new diet while you're busy with all the other activities of life.

**Day One:**

Breakfast: Steel cut oats with a ½ cup of milk and a fried egg.

Lunch: Salmon salad.

Dinner: Grilled or broiled chicken with a ½ cup of penne pasta and stir-fried onions and spinach.

Snack: One pack of Planters heart-healthy nuts.

**Day Two:**

Breakfast: One slice of whole wheat toast with olive oil spread, a ½ cup of cottage cheese (full-fat) and a banana.

Lunch: Turkey sandwich on whole wheat bread, with tomato, lettuce, sliced red onions, a slice of Swiss cheese and olive oil mayo. One orange.

Dinner: Spinach, tomato and avocado salad with balsamic dressing, Chickpea pasta, and a broiled 4-ounce sirloin steak.

Snack: Handful of unsalted sunflower seeds.

**Day Three:**

Breakfast: Small glass of whole milk, peach, and bowl of whole grain cereal.

Lunch: Avocado chickpea salad with penne pasta.

Dinner: Grilled pork chops with pita bread and stir-fried broccoli.

Snack: Apple

**Day Four:**

Breakfast: Whole grain cream of wheat cereal with milk.

Lunch: Avocado with canned sardines and serving of yogurt.

Dinner: Grilled salmon with penne pasta arugula salad.

Snack: Pack of Planters heart-healthy nuts.

**Day Five:**

Breakfast: Fried egg whites on whole grain toast with avocado and a banana.

Lunch: Baked chicken breast with cooked penne pasta in avocado mayo, with one orange.

Dinner: Baked chicken thighs in BBQ sauce with small sweet potato and arugula salad.

Snack: Handful of unsalted walnuts.

**Day Six:**

Breakfast: Steel cut oats with sliced walnuts, 1 tsp. of brown sugar and a ½ cup of milk.

Lunch: Avocado black bean salad.

Dinner: Seared tuna steaks on arugula.

Snack: Two tbsp. of unsalted sunflower seeds.

**Day Seven:**

Breakfast: Fried egg and whole wheat toast.

Lunch: Fried tilapia with couscous and spinach salad.

Dinner: Grilled steak tips with walnut spinach salad and couscous. Orange for dessert.

Snack: Handful of unsalted pecans.

# Chapter 8: Phase Two

In phase two of the diet, which can begin after the first two weeks, we want to ramp up our servings. In phase 2 we will add all the healthy food options you want to include in the diet and form the foundation for a long-term future of health.

## *Transitioning to Phase Two*

For phase two we'll use the following recommendations.

**Dairy**

- Begin making sure that you include 2-3 moderate servings per day of dairy. This can include more than one serving of milk (1/2 cup per serving), a ½ cup of cottage cheese, a ½ cup of unsweetened yogurt, and cheese in 1.5-ounce portions eaten as a snack or used for your recipes.
- If you're lactose intolerant try lactose-free milk or substitute almond or hemp milk.
- Whole milk from grass-fed cows is generally recommended.

- If you drink coffee, you can add a bit of half-and-half if you prefer cream in your coffee.

## Nuts and Seeds

- In phase two, you should eat at least one serving of nuts per day, and you can eat more if your appetite demands it. The key is to avoid overeating. So if you're satisfied, don't eat more. If you eat lunch and are still hungry, then eat ¼ cup of nuts.

## Starchy vegetables

- Limit starchy vegetables like sweet potatoes, potatoes, turnips, and yams to at most one serving per day.

## Fruits

- Our suggestion is to consume adequate fruits, but don't overdo it. While the standard DASH diet allows up to five servings per day, we recommend that you limit your consumption to three servings per day on this diet. It's important to recognize that on the DASH Mediterranean solution diet since you're consuming a lot more fat than you would on the DASH diet alone, you should cut back somewhere else. Cutting back on fruit is a good place to cut because while fruit is generally healthy, it does contain a lot of sugar which will be problematic for some people. You can get all the nutrients you get out of fruits like apples, kiwis, and oranges elsewhere. One possible substitute is a quarter or a half-cup of berries, which have a lower glycemic index and lower carb content than large fruits like apples and bananas. Also, you can get many of the vitamins, minerals, anti-oxidants, and phytonutrients that you get from fruits by consuming large amounts of leafy green vegetables.

- Eat your avocados. The potassium and magnesium in avocados help regulate blood pressure and the monounsaturated fats help make you feel satisfied while promoting heart health. In addition, remember that avocados contain large amounts of fiber that can help with digestive issues.

## *Proportions and Foods for Phase Two*

- 7 servings per day of vegetables, only one of which is a starchy vegetable.
- 3 servings per day of fruit, one of which is an avocado. Also, substitute berries for large sugary fruits.

- 6 servings per day of whole grains. We're cutting back to make room for fat consumption.
- 2-3 moderately sized servings of dairy.
- 2-3 servings of meat (count eggs as meat).
- Olive oil is unlimited. Consume as much as you want to feel satisfied.
- You can introduce some sweets in phase two if desired. Do you really need sweets? You might find that if you abandon sweets after some time passes you rarely crave them.

## *Sample Meal Plan for Phase Two*

### Day One:

Breakfast: 2 fried eggs, one slice of whole grain toast topped with sliced avocado, a ¼ cup of blueberries, one cup of milk.

Lunch: Penne salad with chickpeas in olive-oil mayo, with an orange. Side of a ½ cup of cottage cheese.

Dinner: Broiled salmon, with a ½ cup of couscous in olive oil mixed with chickpeas and cranberries, stir-fried broccoli cooked in olive oil, and stir-fried onions with 1-cup of spinach.

Snack: One pack of Planters heart-healthy nuts.

**Day Two:**

Breakfast: Smoked salmon with avocado, followed by "desert" of strawberries.

Lunch: Chicken with potatoes and asparagus. One serving of yogurt.

Dinner: Ground beef cooked with wild rice and spinach.

Snack: Handful of unsalted walnuts.

**Day Three:**

Breakfast: Small glass of whole milk, a ½ cup of blackberry/raspberry mix, and a bowl of whole grain cereal.

Lunch: Lemon chicken salad.

Dinner: Chicken tacos.

Snack: Can of sardines.

## Day Four:

Breakfast: Whole grain cream of wheat cereal with milk.

Lunch: Garlic mushroom chicken with couscous and spinach avocado salad.

Dinner: Grilled mackerel with couscous, and avocado arugula/tomato salad.

Snack: Handful of unsalted walnuts.

## Day Five:

Breakfast: Fried egg whites on whole grain toast with avocado, a ½ cup of cottage cheese, and a banana.

Lunch: Chicken-orzo salad.

Dinner: Grilled trout with new potatoes and asparagus.

Snack: Handful of unsalted walnuts. Yogurt.

**Day Six:**

Breakfast:  Sardines with avocado.

Lunch: Avocado chickpea salad.

Dinner: Lemon garlic chicken on pasta with stir-fried leafy greens.

Snack: Unsalted walnuts.

**Day Seven:**

Breakfast: Fried egg and whole wheat toast with avocado slices, and a ½ cup of cottage cheese.

Lunch: Fried chicken cubes with couscous and spinach salad, and one serving of yogurt.

Dinner: Broiled trout with wild rice and slivered almond mix, and asparagus. Side of blueberries.

Snack: Handful of unsalted walnuts.

# Chapter 9: Beyond Jumpstarting with the DASH-Mediterranean Solution

By now you've been on the DASH-Mediterranean diet for about one month. You should be completely used to eating using this method and choosing portions and portion sizes should be second nature. Phase two is a trial run for your long term eating plan.

Here are some tips for following the diet long term and tracking progress. The first thing that people should consider is keeping a food diary. Our memories are inherently inaccurate. So writing things down can be important. Especially if you run into a weight loss stall, and you might want to know why you're not progressing. It can be helpful in situations like that to go back to your food diary and see exactly what you've been eating over the past week.

Remember that with the DASH diet or the Mediterranean diet, counting calories isn't something you should be worrying about. So record your food intake by portion sizes (an e.g. ½ cup of cottage cheese, 1 slice of bread).

Now a word about weighing yourself. People are always anxious to see progress, and in today's world of instant gratification, dieters will get frustrated if they step on the scale and they don't see results. The fact is weighing yourself on a daily basis is counter-productive mentally, and on a practical level, it serves no real purpose. It's also a known fact that weight can fluctuate day by day, and it might even have nothing to do with your diet. You might have a bit of water retention one day and show "weight gain".

To avoid these problems we recommend only weighing yourself once per week. Set aside one day per week where you check your weight and note it in your journal. By checking only one day a week (the same day each week by the way), you will avoid the problems of day-to-day fluctuations distorting your view and you can see if you're really making progress.

So what happens if a week goes by and you're not losing weight, or worse, you gained some weight? This is another situation where the diary comes in handy. Are you eating too much? Snacking too much, getting too much fruit? You can get answers to these questions by reading over your diary for the previous week. Be honest with yourself and write down every little thing that you eat so that the information is accurate.

For some people, drinking wine can cause weight loss stall. This will really apply to you if you decide to take up drinking wine on a daily basis when taking up this diet because you've learned that people in the Mediterranean region are washing it down! Remember that wine isn't something that comes without a price – it does have some calories even though they aren't out of this world. If this describes your situation, you may need to adjust a little bit. One strategy, of course, is to cut out the wine or limit your drinking to weekends. However, if you do that it's not clear that you'll get all the benefits that drinking wine has to offer. It seems to be the case that drinking moderate amounts of wine daily provides more health benefits than just drinking a couple of days per week, and even then it's not clear there is any benefit at all.

A second approach to weight loss stall that might be alcohol-related is to cut back a little bit to make room for your wine consumption. This may be cheating a little bit – but you could consider wine to be a serving of fruit. After all, it is made out of crushed grapes, and it has all the antioxidants and important phytonutrients in it that you'd get by eating the grapes. In fact, it's probably very concentrated – how many grapes did it take to make your two glasses of wine?

While the answer to that question may be a deep mystery, counting wine as a fruit when you're on a diet that has 10 servings of fruits and vegetables isn't really all that radical of an idea. The point here is to look somewhere you can cut back. Let's say that typically you're eating

- About 7 servings a day of veggies like leafy greens and broccoli.
- An orange, a banana, and an apple or serving of berries per day.
- Two glasses of wine in the evening.

In this case, you can target the banana for removal. A banana is a sugary fruit, so removing the banana might remove some undesirable sugar-calories. Unfortunately, though, bananas are high in potassium and one of the goals of the DASH-style of eating is to increase your potassium intake. However, you might be surprised that a glass of red wine contains 187 mg of potassium (for a 5 oz. serving). It also provides about 4% of your dietary requirements for magnesium.

Who knew? Well, wine is made out of crushed grapes – so, in fact, it's like drinking grape juice with the sugar removed (in fact the pesky little bugs used to make wine turned the sugar into alcohol for us).

Anyway, since wine contains a significant amount of potassium, giving up the banana isn't going to have too much impact.

As this little exercise shows, we can make trade-offs in our diet when things are not going our way. Be sure to look at everything carefully when you're having weight loss stall to see what kinds of adjustments might help you overcome your lack of progress.

## The Long Term Eating Plan

Your long-term plan on the DASH Mediterranean Diet solution is to follow the advice we've laid out in this book on a daily basis. Studies have shown that the DASH diet impacts blood pressure in as little as two weeks. So if you're choosing this diet for reasons having to do with hypertension or high blood pressure, then after a month it's time to take stock of where you're at. You should monitor your BP regularly. Be sure to measure your blood pressure under similar conditions each time, so that your measurements aren't corrupted by changing environmental conditions. Take your measurements at the same time of day as well.

If your blood pressure is not improving, then examine your diet. Do you need to cut back even more on salt? If you're following the standard DASH diet recommendation of 2,300 mg per day but not seeing results, you may need to reduce your sodium intake to 1,500 mg per day. If you do see results at that point, then you can consider slowly raising your sodium intake on a weekly basis as long as your blood pressure isn't negatively impacted.

### *Keeping it Simple*

While recipes are good, it's not always necessary to pull out some book by a top chef to cook a bang-up recipe. The DASH diet and the Mediterranean diet are both diets that can be approached with simplicity. This is important since it makes it easy to come up with breakfast and lunch ideas that make prepping ahead of time simple and not so time-consuming.

Some suggestions:

- Used canned fish for lunch, breakfast, and snacks. It might strike you as odd to eat fish for breakfast, but that is a very heart-healthy habit to add to your lifestyle. Also canned fish saves time that would otherwise be spent cooking. You can try canned mackerel, canned trout, canned salmon, as well as the old standbys of canned sardines and canned tuna. On the standard DASH diet, they'd tell you to get varieties canned in water, but when combining the DASH diet with the Mediterranean diet fish packed in olive oil isn't just acceptable, it's preferred.
- Look for olive snack packs. Something that's underappreciated is that olives are *fruit* and by eating

actual olives you can get a serving of fruit without packing on sugar. If you visit your local grocery store, you'll see that food companies are selling black and green olives in plastic snack cups. This makes a great addition to your lunch and can help you get even more olive oil.

- Avocado goes with anything. We've tried to drive that thought home when putting together our meal plans. You can put avocado on salad. You can slice it and put it on toast. Avocado is a great addition to a hamburger. In fact, you can just cut it up into cubes, season it and eat it. Also remember that avocado, like olives, is a fruit, not a vegetable.
- Stir-fried greens are easy and pack a lot of nutrients. You can have stir-fried greens with virtually any meal. Since spinach, kale, and arugula basically cook down to nothing when heated over a stove, you can pack 5 servings of the stuff into a single meal. Stir-fried greens don't take up much room, so consider adding them to an omelet, or mixing them up with your favorite pasta.

## *Balancing Macros*

These days "macros" are the entire buzz. What's that about? Macros are just your gross nutrients. So instead of thinking about vitamin and mineral content, macros are the proportions of fat, carbs, and proteins.

Different people respond differently to all the diets out there, and your family history might make you more prone to diabetes or less prone to it. Therefore you might need to make adjustments to the overall diet plan. Here are some clues that this might be the case:

- You're following the general principles of DASH and Mediterranean dieting, you're not overeating, yet you're not losing weight.
- Your blood pressure isn't improving (if this is an issue for you).
- You've been on the diet for a while, and take a blood test, and find you have high triglycerides.
- You have high fasting blood sugars, that aren't improving.

The typical person that might have to readjust their macros (and hence their servings of fruits and whole grains) is probably going to be someone who is pre-diabetic or actually type-2 diabetic. The reason is their body simply doesn't handle carbs very well.

By emphasizing whole grains, the DASH-Mediterranean diet solution will help a lot of people. But some people don't respond even then. But a diet isn't a straight jacket. If you need to make adjustments, then make adjustments. The key is to begin cutting back on whole grains and fruits and replacing them with fat. We aren't saying to adapt the keto diet, but some people may end up there. What we are suggesting is to slowly cut back and replace. We've already made some suggestions for using avocado and olives for your fruits. If you are having trouble, then you might want to eliminate sweet fruit entirely and only consume avocados and olives. Believe it – if you're eating avocados and lots of leafy greens, you're getting all the fruits and vegetables your body needs. This can be done in a couple of steps because not all fruits have the same amount of carbohydrate content or the same glycemic index. So you might start out replacing that banana and watermelon with some blueberries and blackberries. If that still doesn't work out, then move to replace the berries with olives. It doesn't have to be a complete replacement. You can replace one of your three daily servings of fruit with olives or avocado and see how it works out.

Cutting back on bread and other whole grains can also help many people that have problems digesting sugars. If you're currently at 7 servings of whole grains but having trouble losing weight, consider cutting back to 4 servings – but make up the calories with fat and some protein.

# Chapter 10: Breakfast Recipes

## Avocado and Poached Egg Toast with Salmon

Ingredients

- 2 slices of whole grain toast
- 2 poached eggs
- 4 ounces of smoked salmon
- Avocado slices
- 1/4 tsp freshly squeezed lemon juice
- Salt and pepper to taste
- 1 tbsp. of sliced scallions

Instructions

- Cook two poached eggs.
- Mash avocado in a small bowl with a fork. Add a bit of lemon juice and a pinch of salt. Add scallions and mix.
- Toast two slices of whole grain bread. Spread liberally with avocado then top off with smoked salmon.
- Place a poached egg onto each slice of toast.

# Baked Eggs with Avocado and Feta Cheese

Ingredients

- 1 avocado
- 4 eggs
- 3 tbsp. of crumbled feta cheese
- Avocado slices
- 1/4 tsp freshly squeezed lemon juice
- Salt and pepper to taste

Instructions

- Preheat oven to 400 degrees.
- Cut avocado into slices and line two baking bowls with it. Crack your eggs and place 2 eggs into each bowl. Salt and pepper to taste.
- Sprinkle with feta cheese. Bake for about 12 minutes.
- Serve with a slice of whole grain toast and a ½ cup of cottage cheese on the side.

Roasted Roma Tomato Breakfast Sandwich

Ingredients

- Whole grain ciabatta roll

- ¼ cup of egg whites
- 1 tsp. chopped basil
- 1 tbsp. pesto
- 2 slices provolone cheese
- About ½ cup roasted tomatoes (recipe below)
- 4-5 grape tomatoes
- 1 tbsp. extra virgin olive oil
- Black pepper to taste

Instructions

1. Preheat oven to 400 degrees.
2. Slice tomatoes in half, place on a baking sheet and drizzle with olive oil and season with black pepper.
3. Roast tomatoes for 15-20 minutes.
4. Put a tsp. of olive oil into a skillet over medium heat. Add egg whites to the pan, seasoning with black pepper and chopped basil. Cook until the egg is done, flipping to get both sides. Just before removing from pan, place the slices of provolone cheese on top, and let it melt slightly.
5. Toast the ciabatta bread. Then spread both sides with pesto and place the egg on one half. Place the roasted tomatoes on top of the melted cheese.

# Mediterranean Scrambled Eggs

Ingredients

- 3 eggs
- 1 tbsp. extra-virgin olive oil
- 1/3 cup diced tomato
- 1 cup baby spinach
- 2 tbsp. feta cheese, cubed
- Black pepper to taste

Instructions

- Sauté tomatoes and spinach in a skillet with the olive oil over medium heat.
- Add eggs and scramble.
- Cook to desired doneness.
- Season to taste.

# Egg toast with salsa and avocado

Ingredients

- 1-2 eggs
- 1 slice of whole grain toast
- 1 tbsp. of olive oil
- ½ avocado
- 2 tbsp. of hot salsa
- Black pepper and garlic powder to taste

Instructions

- Mash together your avocado with the salsa. Season with black pepper and garlic powder.
- Toast one slice of whole grain bread.
- In a small nonstick skillet, cook an egg, style as desired.
- Place egg on toast and top off with 1-2 tsp. of salsa.

## Mushroom-Egg Omelet

Ingredients

- ½ cup of sliced mushrooms
- 1 tbsp. of olive oil
- ¼ cup of chopped green onions
- 3 grape tomatoes, halved

Instructions

- Stir-fry mushrooms and onions over medium heat in 1 tbsp. of olive oil. Set aside when done.
- Beat egg in a bowl together with salt and pepper to taste
- Add cherry tomatoes and pour in fried mushroom mixture.
- Pour egg into skillet and cook over medium heat.

## Mediterranean Breakfast Bowl

Ingredients

- 4 cooked eggs, as desired.
- 1 avocado, cut in thin slices.
- 1 ½ cup of cooked quinoa.
- A handful of sliced almonds.
- 5-10 asparagus stalks, cut in 1-inch pieces.
- 3 cups of arugula.
- Olive oil and vinegar dressing.
- ½ cup of hummus.
- 2 tsp. of Dijon mustard.

Instructions

- Sauté asparagus in a skillet over medium heat. Set aside when done.
- Toss arugula with dressing in a bowl.
- Add cooked asparagus and quinoa, and mix.
- Place hummus in a bowl and smear along sides.
- Put arugula mixture into a bowl.
- Top with avocado slices, and then eggs.
- Finish off with sliced almonds.

# Chapter 11: Beef and Pork Recipes

## Beef with wild rice

Ingredients

- A ½ pound of ground beef
- 3 cups of cooked wild rice
- 2 chopped green onions
- 1 diced red bell pepper
- 1 diced yellow onion
- 2 diced celery stalks
- 2 cloves of minced garlic
- 2 tsp. of Worcestershire sauce
- 1 2/2 tsp. of thyme
- ½ tsp. of marjoram
- 1 tsp. of basil
- black pepper to taste
- 1 cup of water

Instructions

- Heat a skillet over medium heat, Place the ground beef, yellow onion, and celery in the pan and cook for about 5 minutes.

- Add Worcestershire sauce, herbs, chopped bell pepper, green onion, and water. Stir mixture and bring to a boil.
- Reduce heat to a simmer and cook for 20 minutes.
- Remove from heat and mix together with the wild rice.

# Sliced Flank Steak with Couscous Salad

## Ingredients

- 1 flank steak
- 1 cup whole wheat couscous
- 1 cup Zucchini, cut into 1/4-inch pieces
- 1 bell pepper, cut into 1/4-inch pieces
- 1/2 cup finely chopped yellow onion
- 1/2 tsp. ground cumin
- 1/2 tsp. ground black pepper
- 1/2 cup olive oil and vinegar dressing
- 1 tbsp. of olive oil
- 1 tbsp. of chopped basil

## Directions

- Cook couscous according to directions.
- While couscous is cooking, grill or broil the flank steak. Cut into thin slices.
- In a large bowl, add couscous and other ingredients. Toss thoroughly to mix. Place salad mixture on plates, and top off with slices of steak. Season to taste with black pepper and garlic powder.

# Beef with Olives and Feta Cheese

Ingredients

- 2 pounds of lean beef stew meat, cut into cubes

- 1 cup of green olives, pitted and sliced
- 4 Roma tomatoes, cut in quarters
- Black pepper and garlic powder to taste
- ½ cup of feta cheese, crumbled
- 1 package of couscous, cooked according to directions.

Instructions

- Add ingredients to a slow cooker and mix well.
- Cover and cook on high for 5-6 hours.
- Season with black pepper and garlic salt.
- Stir well and serve over couscous.

# Chapter 12: Poultry Recipes

## Baked Chicken Thighs with brown rice

### Ingredients

- 1 pound boneless, skinless chicken thighs
- 3/4 cup brown rice
- 1 cup dry white wine
- 1 cup of chopped green onions
- 2 cups unsalted chicken broth
- 1 cup of chopped celery
- 1 tsp. fresh tarragon
- Garlic powder and black pepper to taste

### Directions

- Preheat oven to 300 degrees.
- Place the brown rice, 1 cup of broth, and white wine into a glass baking dish.
- Grab a baking dish and add 1 cup of broth, the white wine, and your rice. Let sit for 20 minutes or so to let the rice absorb the liquid.
- Lightly season chicken with garlic powder and black pepper.

- Cut chicken thighs into 1-inch strips. Over medium heat in a nonstick frying pan with one tbsp. of olive oil, add the chicken thigh meat. Then add onions, celery, tarragon, and half of the unsalted broth. Cook for around 10 minutes.
- Place the mixture in the baking dish. Cover and bake for 30 minutes.

# Grilled Chicken Breast with lemon and arugula

Ingredients:

- 2 boneless, skinless chicken breasts
- 2 cups of arugula
- A handful of cherry tomatoes, sliced in half
- 1 tsp. of lemon juice
- 1 tbsp. of olive oil
- 1 tsp. of Capers or more to taste
- Black pepper and garlic powder

Directions:

- Season chicken to taste.
- Broil chicken in the oven.
- Place the arugula on a plate. Top off with tomatoes.
- Slice the broiled chicken into longitudinal slices and place on top of the salad.
- Drizzle with olive oil and lemon juice.

# Stir-fried Chicken thighs with Hummus

Ingredients:

- Two chicken thighs, but into cubes
- Package of baby spinach
- Two cans of garbanzo beans (chickpeas)
- 2 tbsp. of tahini
- 1/3 cup of fresh lemon juice
- 1 cup of yogurt of your choice
- 3 cloves of garlic

Directions:

- Season chicken thighs with black pepper and garlic powder.
- Heat pan over medium heat, with a liberal amount of extra virgin olive oil.
- Stir fry chicken until nearly done.
- Add package of baby spinach and cook until wilted.
- Place garbanzo beans, tahini, lemon juice, yogurt, and garlic in a food processor or blender.
- Mix until smooth, but maintain a thick consistency

- Pour into the frying pan and mix together with chicken and spinach.

# Chapter 13: Fish and Seafood

## Seared Tuna and Arugula Salad

Ingredients:

- 2 tuna steaks
- 2 cups of arugula
- 1 tsp. of lemon juice
- One tbsp. of extra-virgin olive oil
- A handful of cherry tomatoes, sliced
- 1 tsp. of Capers
- Black pepper to taste

Directions:

1. Season tuna steaks with pepper to taste.
2. Preheat a frying pan on high heat.
3. Sear tuna on both sides for 60-90 seconds per side.
4. Place the arugula on a plate with tomatoes and capers.
5. Slice your tuna into longitudinal slices and place on top of the arugula.

6. Drizzle with olive oil and lemon juice.

# Octopus with Couscous

Ingredients:

- Octopus
- Package of whole grain couscous
- 3 tbsp. olive oil
- 10-12 Grape tomatoes, sliced
- 2 tbsp. chopped garlic
- 1/2 tsp. dried hot red pepper flakes
- 1/4 cup chopped parsley
- 2 tbsp. chopped fresh basil

Directions:

1. Cook octopus as desired.
2. Sauté garlic and red pepper flakes in oil in a frying pan using medium-high heat.
3. Add parsley and basil with tomatoes and stir fry for about a minute.
4. Add octopus and cook until very tender, about 45 minutes to 1 hour. Season with garlic powder and pepper.
5. Cook Couscous according to directions.

6. Place couscous on serving plates and pour octopus sauce on top.

# Broiled Trout with Wild Rice

Ingredients

- 2 4-ounce trout fillets
- One package of couscous.
- 1 tsp. of minced garlic
- No-salt herb seasoning of your choice, to taste
- 1 tbsp. lemon juice
- 1 tsp. garlic, minced
- Ground black pepper, to taste

Directions

- Preheat broiler, positioning rack about 4 inches from heat source.
- Season trout fillets to taste using black pepper and herb blend, and place skin side down in the pan.
- Drizzle with olive oil and lemon juice and add garlic.
- Broil for about 10 minutes until fish flakes easily.
- Cook couscous as directed, and serve.

# Chapter 14: 7 Healthy Desserts

## Chocolate Mousse

Ingredients

- 3/4 cup milk
- 2 cups of yogurt
- 4 ounces of chocolate
- 1 tbsp. of honey
- 1/2 tsp. vanilla extract

Instructions

- Finely chop the chocolate.
- Pour milk into a saucepan and add chocolate.
- Gently heat until chocolate melts, do not boil.
- Once combined, incorporate honey and your vanilla extract
- Scoop yogurt into a large bowl.
- Pour the chocolate and milk mixture on top.
- Mix well before transferring to individual bowls.
- Chill in the refrigerator for 2 hours. Before serving, top off each bowl with a spoonful of yogurt.

# Chocolate Mascarpone

Ingredients:

- 8 ounces of Mascarpone cheese
- 8 ounces of white chocolate
- 4 ounces of semisweet dark chocolate
- 1 cup of Greek Yogurt
- 3 tbsp. of sugar
- 1 tsp. of grated orange peel
- ¼ tsp. of vanilla extract
- White chocolate curls

Directions:

- Finely chop your white and dark chocolate.
- Line muffin cups with paper liners.
- Using a double boiler melts white chocolate and then spoon into each lined muffin cup.
- Freeze for half an hour until chocolate is firm.
- Use remaining melted white chocolate to form a second layer of white chocolate over the first one laid down.
- Freeze a second time, for one hour.
- Melt the dark chocolate in a double boiler.
- Set aside and allow cooling.

- Add yogurt and sugar into a large bowl and mix thoroughly.
- Mix melted dark chocolate, orange peel, vanilla, and cheese together using an electric mixer.
- Mix for about 30 seconds.
- Fold the yogurt and sugar mixture in the chocolate.
- Remove your muffin cups from the freezer and add the chocolate and yogurt mixture to each muffin cup.
- Add white chocolate curls to the top of each dessert cup.
- Can be served or saved overnight in the refrigerator. If stored, allow warming to room temperature about an hour before serving.

## Greek yogurt and Peanut Butter

Ingredients

- 4 cups Greek yogurt
- ¼ cup of creamy peanut butter
- ¼ cup of flaxseed meal
- 2 bananas, sliced
- 1 tsp. of nutmeg

Instructions

- Divide yogurt into four serving bowls.
- Top off with banana slices.

- Melt peanut butter.
- Drizzle peanut butter on top of bananas.
- Mix nutmeg into flaxseed meal.
- Sprinkle the flaxseed mixture on top of the peanut butter.

# Almond Ricotta Spread

Ingredients

- 1 cup of ricotta cheese
- ½ cup of sliced almonds
- Tsp. of honey
- Orange zest
- ¼ tsp. of almond extract
- Sliced toasted whole wheat bread

Instructions

- Place ricotta cheese and sliced almonds in a mixing bowl and gently stir together.
- Add almond extract and honey and mix further.
- Transfer to a serving bowl. Sprinkle top with more sliced almonds and drizzle with a tsp. of honey.
- When serving, apply liberal amounts to the toasted bread.

# Chocolate Avocado Pudding

Ingredients

- ¼ cup of melted chocolate chips
- ¼ cup of cocoa powder
- 4 tbsp. of whole milk
- 2 avocados
- 1/2 tsp. pure vanilla extract.
- ¼ cup of sugar

Instructions

- Combine all ingredients in a blender or food processor until completely smooth.

# Baklava with lemon-honey syrup

Ingredients

- 1 lb. of chopped nuts (almonds, walnuts, or pistachios are best, or use a combination of them)
- 1 lb. of phyllo dough
- 1 cup of butter, melted
- 1/3 cup of sugar
- 1 tsp. of ground cinnamon
- 1/3 tsp. of ground cloves

*Syrup:*

- 1 cup of water
- 1 cup of sugar
- 1/2 cup of honey
- 2 tbsp. of lemon juice
- 1 cinnamon stick

Instructions (courtesy of simplyrecipes.com)

- Grease a 9x13 pan and set the oven to 350°F.
- Thaw the phyllo dough according to manufacturer's directions (this may take overnight). When thawed, roll out the dough and cut the dough in half so the sheets will fit in the pan. Cover with a damp towel to keep it from drying out.

- Crush nuts until in small, even sized pieces. Mix with sugar, cinnamon, and cloves. In a separate bowl, melt the butter in the microwave.
- Place a sheet of phyllo dough into the pan. Using a pastry brush, brush the phyllo sheet with melted butter. Repeat 7 more times until it is 8 sheets thick, each sheet being "painted" with the butter.
- Smooth on a thin layer of the nut mixture. Cover with two more sheets of phyllo, brushing each one with butter. Continue to repeat the nut mixture and two buttered sheets of phyllo until the nut mixture is all used up. The top layer should be 8 phyllo sheets thick; each sheet being individually buttered. Do not worry if the sheets crinkle up a bit, it will just add more texture.
- Cut into 24 equal sized squares using a sharp knife. Bake at 350°F for 30-35 minutes or until lightly golden brown and edges appear slightly crisp.
- While baking, make the syrup. Combine the cinnamon stick, sugar, lemon juice, honey, and water in a saucepan. Bring to a boil, then reduce to medium-low heat and let simmer for 7 minutes and slightly thickened. Remove the cinnamon stick and allow to cool.

- Spoon the cooled syrup over the hot baklava and let cool for at least 4 hours. Garnish with some finely crushed pistachios if desired.

# Kourabiedes Greek Butter Cookies

Ingredients

- 1 egg
- 1 pound of unsalted butter
- 1 ½ cup of powdered sugar
- 5 cups of whole wheat flour
- 1/8 tsp. of baking soda
- ¼ tsp. of salt
- 1 tbsp. of almond extract

Instructions

- Preheat oven to 350 degrees.
- Beat butter in mixer on medium-high speed for 20 minutes.
- Add egg to butter mixture together with almond extract, mix until thoroughly combined.
- Sift ½ cup powdered sugar, baking soda, flour, and salt together in a large bowl.
- With the speed on low, add mixture a little bit at a time until completely mixed.
- To make cookies get 2 tbsp. of the mixture for each cookie.
- Form into crescents and place on a baking sheet lined with parchment.

- Bake for 18-20 minutes until lightly browned and cooked through.
- Toss in powdered sugar after cooling slightly.
- Serve warm.

# Conclusion

Thank you for reading the DASH Diet – Mediterranean solution! We hope that you have found this book entertaining and most of all informative. Remember that good health is a lifelong process and a journey. Don't despair when you slip up on occasion, just climb back on board.

The DASH diet was originally designed to help patients with hypertension manage their blood pressure without having to use medications. Although it wasn't designed for weight loss, patients found that they did lose weight while following the diet. The DASH diet doesn't use calorie counting or any complicated point systems. Instead, food portions are measured and there are simple rules for daily portions.

The DASH diet is based on a pyramid, with the most frequently consumed items as the base. That would be fruits and vegetables. These items are supposed to be consumed liberally, in servings of 8-10 per day, with 4-5 servings of vegetables and 4-5 servings of fruits. Next, 6-8 servings of whole grains are to be eaten daily. While 2-3 servings of dairy are to be consumed per day, meat is eaten in relative moderation. Only lean cuts of skinless poultry and fish are eaten regularly in 3-4 ounce portions. Oils are allowed only in tiny amounts, and nuts with at most 1 serving per day.

The DASH diet was originally developed in the early 1990s. Back then, ideas about the role of fat in the diet were quite different than they are today. In those times it was believed that fat was the cause of heart disease and stroke, and so doctors sought to promote very low-fat diets. Since that time, however, doctors have learned that the role of fat in the diet is far more complicated than originally believed. In fact, fat with the exception of a small number of bad fats is good for health. Furthermore, fat actually helps dieters refrain from overeating, because it leaves you feeling satiated and full of energy.

The Mediterranean diet isn't really a diet, it's simply the traditional way of eating in the Mediterranean region. Living very close to the sea, fish has long been a staple food of people living in the coastal regions of Spain, Portugal, France, Italy, Greece, and other countries. It has been known for a long time that people in these countries don't suffer from chronic diseases at the same rates that westerners do. In particular, rates of heart disease are quite low in these countries.

Researchers soon noted that the Mediterranean diet actually included a large amount of fat. However, it was mostly unsaturated fat and fish oils. While there are some similarities to the DASH diet, the Mediterranean diet only provides suggestions of what to consume and doesn't give specific portions. This is because it's not a diet that has been designed by doctors, it's just a traditional cuisine.

The "pyramid" of the Mediterranean diet also has fruits and vegetables at the base, topped by whole grains like the DASH diet. However, there is no specification on how many servings to consume, basically, you eat until you're full. Meat can be consumed daily along with beans and legumes. Fish is consumed quite liberally at least twice per week, but often more than that. Avocados, which are consumed in strict moderation on the DASH diet because of its high-fat content, are eaten liberally on the Mediterranean diet. In addition, nuts can also be consumed liberally on the Mediterranean diet, and oils are consumed in abundance, but that would be specifically olive oil.

The fats of the Mediterranean diet offer benefits to heart health that a low-fat diet like the DASH diet doesn't offer. However, the Mediterranean diet doesn't include the benefits for blood pressure that the DASH diet does. Therefore combining the two together to form a new diet can bring the best of both to create a new, better diet.

That has been the goal of this book. We have described a new combination of the two diets that help you get the heart-healthy fats found in fish, avocadoes, and olive oil together with the balance and limited sodium of the DASH diet. By combining the two together, you can reduce all of your risk factors associated with cardiovascular disease.

Why do this? Why not just stick to the Mediterranean diet? The reason is that high blood pressure is an independent risk factor for heart disease and stroke. That is, you can have low cholesterol, low triglycerides, high HDL, be thin and exercise, but if you have high blood pressure, you're still at elevated risk for having a heart attack or stroke. Controlling high blood pressure is one of the most important things you can do for your health.

Adding fat to the diet will help control diabetes, which may be the scourge of our time when it comes to public health concerns. The DASH diet really isn't suitable for dealing with diabetes, because low-fat diets are not really the best approach to use. Most people with pre-diabetes or diagnosed type-2 diabetes will find that even eating whole grains, or fruit, they will get blood sugar spikes. They will also probably find that following a low-fat diet like DASH, while it may help them control their weight and blood pressure, it won't do much to control their blood sugar. Here the Mediterranean diet steps in, with the high-fat content those with a tendency toward developing diabetes will find themselves having much better results. Those who are pre-diabetic may be able to avoid becoming full-blown type 2 diabetics. If you are already diagnosed with diabetes, without offering false hope, it is possible that following a strict version of the diet as outlined in this book may help you reduce or even get off your medications. This is something that you should discuss with your doctor.

The diet may also have dramatic effects on blood pressure. This can't be predicted ahead of time; some people are going to be more sensitive to salt than others. If you have high blood pressure and the diet isn't helping lower it, then adapt the low-sodium version of the DASH diet, which limits total sodium intake to 1,500 mg per day. If you are on blood pressure medication, this is something that you will need to discuss with your doctor before doing.

The DASH diet and the Mediterranean diet are both designed for long-term health. They can be considered more of a lifestyle than a diet. Don't be afraid to make adjustments to your eating plans as necessary to attain optimum health. We wish you the best of luck on your journey toward health and weight loss.

Printed in Great Britain
by Amazon